LIVING IN THE MOURNING LIGHT

by

Andrea Corrie

Published by Exmoor News
www.exmoornews.co.uk

EXMOOR
NEWS

James in Brighton

Reviewers' Comments

"I first met Andrea in February 2016, at the launch of the UK Drowning Prevention Strategy; for me, that event was the culmination of a few years' hard work with colleagues from partner agencies who sat on the National Water Safety Forum's co-ordinating Group. It had been our job to support the development of the strategy, but for Andrea it was so much more than that.

As a senior officer in a blue light service (Fire and Rescue) I volunteered in 2013 to take on a national role for our professional body: then CFOA (the Chief Fire Officers Association) and now called the National Fire Chiefs Council (NFCC), to lead in the UK in our sector for Water Rescue and Drowning Prevention and help support Fire and Rescue Services to engage and support prevention and education work. I had seen how effective our sector contribution could be to reduce other sorts of accidents and emergencies such as Fire and Road accidents and it was important that those that respond to emergencies engaged. Prevention is, after all, better than cure.

What struck me about that meeting with Andrea, and indeed the many other families that I have worked with over the years, is the strength of their motivation to prevent any other family going through what they have experienced.

Andrea told her family's story about the loss of her son, James, with dignity and also with love. As a mother myself, some of her words resonated with me on a deeper level than my professional role. I already knew how important parents' voices are as advocates for prevention and at that moment, I knew Andrea could help move hearts as well as minds on this vitally important issue.

Since February 2016 I have met and spoken with Andrea many times. I invited her to East Sussex to speak to a group of staff about her journey and to help them reflect on how we should approach our water safety work. I was very grateful when she came with her husband. I also asked her to help with contribution to a national professional film for Fire and Rescue Services as part of the *NFCC Be Water Aware* campaign, again to give a parent's perspective, and she has contributed so much to the work of the RNLI as James's story features so prominently in the Respect the Water campaign.

In my professional view, it is critical that we collaborate and work in partnership to reduce drownings. We are many voices together, with different perspectives, yet the same goal: to improve water safety in the UK."

Dawn Whittaker *CFO and CEO of East Sussex Fire and Rescue Service and UK National Fire Chiefs Council Lead for Water Safety and Drowning Prevention*

"Andrea Corrie's commitment to water safety education since losing James is both motivating and humbling. We met in 2014, and I've had the pleasure of working with her on many occasions since, listening to her bravely sharing James's tragic story to try and help others avoid the heart-breaking experience of losing a loved one to drowning. Although I never had the pleasure of meeting James, I know he'd be extremely proud of everything she's achieved in his memory."

Ross Macleod, *Manager, RNLI*

"*Living in the Mourning Light* is, in essence, the completion of a journey. A rather special, emotional journey that only a mother who has lost a child can make and understand. *Into the Mourning Light* was the start of the journey and explores the rollercoaster of emotions experienced by a grieving mother, whilst *Living in the Mourning Light* is a confirmation that it is possible to emerge from that dark tunnel of despair, revitalised and ready to continue with life.

However, Andrea's books are not limited to just those who have lost a child. They provide valuable insights to anyone who has experienced the passing of a loved one and also, just as importantly, explain how to offer advice and guidance to such people by putting yourself in their place and empathising with their situation. As anyone who has lost parents, a spouse and other loved ones along the way, both of these books can help you to understand and recognise the various stages of grief and how you can emerge as a stronger and more fulfilled person at the end of the process.

Personally, as someone who has recently experienced the passing of a loving wife of over thirty years, it has shown me that mourning the loss of a loved one acts as a valuable lesson in realising how precious life is and how we should make the most of every day we spend here. Otherwise one day we might look back and regret it!"

Geoff Clamp, *Hallmark Financial Planning Ltd*

"As a bereaved mum myself, and a volunteer for The Compassionate Friends, I found Andrea's first book *Into the Mourning Light* helped me and others as we struggle with the all-encompassing grief we feel for our children. Reading about the feelings and the experiences of somebody who has suffered such a traumatic loss, and has survived, can provide you with the hope that you can survive too, as impossible as that might seem in the beginning. I was, therefore, very pleased and excited to hear that Andrea was writing a second book, and that she intended to specifically focus on the hope, not only of survival but of a return to a meaningful life; a life which allows you to feel happiness, and even joy, again. I think that's something that will not only help those of us who are grieving for our beloved children, but everyone who is grieving for someone they love dearly, as well as those who are trying to support us."

Mary Hartley, *Librarian, The Compassionate Friends*

About the Author

Having lived and worked in Surrey for most of her life, Andrea and her husband Shaun heeded the call of the South West and moved to Mid Devon in 2017. They enjoy exploring the beautiful countryside, often walking with Shadow, their rescue greyhound. Andrea continues to work part of the week as a medical secretary at a local GP practice. In her free time, she likes to record life with a camera and a pen and relishes being able to chase round after grandchildren, cook elaborate recipes and generally celebrate a stage of life not entirely governed by the clock.

Keep in Touch!

Andrea welcomes feedback on her writing and can be emailed at
andrea.corrie@outlook.com
She writes a blog entitled *Multi-layered Musings of New Normality* at
https://andreacorriesblog.wordpress.com/

For my wonderful children:

Stella Louise Gardener (nee Clark)

And

James Edward Clark

And for all the others who make a difference.

Poem for My Son

Listen for him
In the ripple of the breeze
Among the rustling of the trees
Listen – and you will surely hear
An echo of his voice, so dear

Pick him out
In the swirling crowd
His set of shoulders, standing proud
See a turn of head, glimpse blonde hair
Those bright blue eyes and smile so fair

Listen to his music
Though it may not be your taste
The beat is fast, like a life in haste
The lyrics repeat a story well told
But he will not know of growing old

Talk to him
Reminisce his childish ways
Tell him how you fill your days
Now he is no longer present
Not idly but in time well spent

Eat his favourite meal
A homage to his days
The table has an empty place
But you must eat and nourish
So in his absence, you thrive and flourish

Tread his path
Do not be afraid to walk
Where he walked; talk
Of him and share his track
Now understanding there's no turning back

Remember him
Hold close each of those precious years
Feel the cleansing of your tears
Smile and move forward, joyful and bright
Honour him; by living in the mourning light.

Andrea Corrie   January 2016

Foreword

Andrea is my dear friend and I feel very honoured to have her in my life, even though it was death that brought us together. Not one death, but two. The deaths of two wonderful, unique, nineteen-year-old boys, three years apart. Those boys are our sons, James and Tom.

Andrea reached out to me in 2009, after she read about my loss through the charity The Compassionate Friends.

I was a year into the devastation of traumatic child loss. Andrea was compassionate and kind. She listened. We walked. We talked. We cried.

As our association and subsequent friendship grew, many coincidences were revealed. Our boys had gone to the same primary school. We must at times have stood shoulder to shoulder in the school grounds at the end of the day or at school events. We lived around the corner to each other and walked the same route to school. We shopped in the same places.

However, we were not destined to meet then. We were to wait until 2009.

The more I get to know Andrea the deeper my respect for her grows. My admiration for her positivity and generosity in helping others is huge. She strives to ensure that other families do not suffer the same pain and loss that she lives with. Her safety campaign has altered the riverside at Kingston for the greater good, because of her concern for others and her determination to make it safer.

The Royal National Lifeboat Institution has recognised Andrea's work toward drowning prevention with a national award, and she continues to play an active role in getting her message across through the RNLI and Fire and Rescue services.

Andrea does so much more than that, though. Through her writing and her blog, her words and wisdom reach more people than we can possibly imagine. Through insightful reflection of her own journey with loss, and through her interaction with others similarly affected, she has accumulated a considerable number of tools, both practical and holistic, that can be helpful. Not everyone can articulate their grief or their feelings, but I know first-hand that her words are helpful, calming and often healing.

We cannot change the past but, we can decide how we choose to live life moving forward. Andrea's first book, *Into the Mourning Light*, charted those first steps, those faltering forays in the mourning light as we sought to process all that had happened, and all that we had lost, and the discovery of hope.

Living in the Mourning Light continues the narrative, confirming that being able to live a life that is meaningful and positive, is possible. Through losing our sons, we both understand how it is to live in the presence of absence.

Andrea's text is honest and heart-warming, openly acknowledging that there are moments that are bittersweet; times when great joy is tempered by great loss. She finds contentment in the beauty around her, the miracles of nature and the human spirit, and she draws strength from her spiritual faith.

Andrea is an inspiration to us all, and her words, inspired by James, are a gift to us all.

Linda Sewell

Introduction

Throughout this book, the descriptors of Hope, Light, Love, Faith and Resilience are the main characters. I know them well and I draw on them as you would draw on friends. I share their attributes with the intention of helping others in grief.

The story is the inter-weaving of the insights that accompany me as I live in the mourning light. Individually and collectively, these would not have come about in such strength of form, were it not for my loss. They are not consolation for loss, but they are comfort for the future. They affirm that I live mindfully and meaningfully despite losing my son James to accidental drowning in 2005.

The insights have separate attributes but they share a commonality: they represent the positive outcome of a great deal of grieving work, soul-searching, thought, rumination, prayer, meditation, focus, introspection, examination, cross-examination, talking, listening and writing.

No wonder they are like strong personalities in their own right!

I was asked recently:

"How do you think your life would have differed had James not died in 2005?"

I am sure that I would not have crossed paths with such an extraordinary number of inspiring, courageous people over the intervening years. The question encourages me to reflect on past events and I realise how things have changed; through the people I've met, the challenges I've overcome, the emotions I have experienced and above all how much richer my tapestry of life has become because of these contributing factors. Most importantly, with everything that has gone before, I am now ready ... physically, mentally, spiritually and emotionally, to carry on with the rest of my life.

Those people who knew James throughout his life: his family, colleagues, peers and friends; recognise that I welcome mention of him and I reiterate that I am always happy to talk about him. I am lucky to have loyal friends who understand much about my grief and continue to offer their unstinting support whenever it is needed. It is a common error for people not to mention the name of the person who died. Years ago, a death in the family would have been brushed under the carpet and hardly referred to once the funeral was over.

I like to think that we live in more enlightened times and cannot stress enough the value of getting grief out into the open, examining it and talking through it as positively as possible.

As I wrote in *Into the Mourning Light* I have learned much about moving from a dark place to a light place and I am thankful to walk in the mourning light; it is not quite the same as the 'before bereavement' light, but it is pretty close. It is true that grief itself dims with time. The light that is the essence of our spirit and our being continues to shine brighter and brighter until it breaks through the darkness.

Today, after these years of loss, I can share the optimism that comes from a life full of new connections, exciting beginnings and a truly positive thought process, all of which reflect how it is possible to come out of the darkest despondency of grief into the suffused brilliance and the quiet joy of the mourning light. After all these years, I understand that the light holds tensile strength in its glow and reflectivity.

I hope that individually and collectively, the insights about which I write offer you the same sense of support, encouragement and upliftment that I experience.

Chapter 1

Introducing Hope

Here is Hope.

If you visualise her as a person, she stands in the corner surrounded by an opaque light that gradually becomes brighter and clearer the longer it is observed.

Hope stands with both feet planted firmly on the ground. Her arms outstretched she emits a compassionate sense of warmth that beckons.

Look hard for Hope. Not always seen, but always there.

Hope is the comforter of mankind, one of her historical embodiments being a Greek goddess who carries flowers in her arms. Elpis, the spirit of Hope, was said to be left behind in Pandora's Box after all the mayhem and chaos was released. It is interesting that her opposite number is Moros, the spirit of hopelessness and doom. What is grief if it is not doom? Early grief looks black and endless and a successful pathway along the route through mourning and grieving can only work with a positive attitude and a gathering of hope for the future. Hope must be drawn around us like a protective cloak to become one of the first key elements that can move us forward in our pain and loss. There is no secret recipe for successful grieving. Our path will be as uniquely individual as our handwriting

1

or the rings of a tree trunk, but hope is intrinsic to success. Finding hope for a meaningful time to come in the future, when we are newly bereaved, is perhaps one of the most difficult things to achieve. Where is hope's evidence? Hope's evidence lies in the results of that driving force that enables us to move forward even when we think we cannot.

Where are hope's examples that will spur us on to embrace a positive and optimistic future?

Emily Dickinson's poem[1] says:

Hope is the thing with feathers
That perches in the soul,
And sings the tune without the words,
And never stops at all,
And sweetest in the gale is heard;
And sore must be the storm
That could abash the little bird
That kept so many warm.

I've heard it in the chillest land,
And on the strangest sea;
Yet, never, in extremity,
It asked a crumb of me.

The truth of hope lies in the fact that hope asks nothing

of us.

Hope is like a well-meaning friend.

Hope is our natural expectation that, in the darkest of times, things will get better, not worse.

Hope is honest, holding the belief that there are brighter days ahead.

Hope is an innate gift of the spirit rather than something that can be learned.

We have all had days that start with a flat tyre, a traffic jam, a missed train … things that set us off wrong-footed from the start. But usually, we can rationalise these events and say,

"Oh well, it doesn't matter, the day can only get better," and generally, it does.

But such a premise is outside the remit of the newly bereaved.

Stunned and numb, we cannot look for hope. We are hope-less, not hope-full.

We are helpless in the absence of hope, buffeted this way and that by the emotions that accompany death and grieving. None of these feelings are positive. They are dark, despondent, depressing, demoralising emotions that knock out hope. They are incredibly hard to face, let alone deal with. They drag us down; they do not lift us up.

We cannot see beyond the next breath, the next second, the next minute, the next hour, the next day. We have lost hope with the death of our loved one. We are at the nadir, the very bottom of the pit of the worst and most fearful of emotions. We feel as though we are alone in the darkness. We have to point ourselves towards life and living even as we experience the lonely, foreign environs to which, without a recognisable compass, grief has sent us.

How, then, do we recover this nebulous thing called hope? We are hard-wired to optimism. It is in our human psyche. But death temporarily removes our normal responses. Our positive emotions are dulled in the face of the negative inward shrieking that accompanies loss. We are quite unable to grasp the finality of loss in one go.

Recovering hope does not happen overnight. Like most targets of the grieving process, we have to work at it to get it back.

Paulo Coelho says[2], *"You don't choose your life: it chooses you. There's no point asking why life has reserved certain joys and griefs; you just accept them and carry on. We can't choose our lives, but we can decide what to do with the joys or griefs we're given."*

I was struck by this quote when I read it. But on closer examination, I see it as contradictory. On one hand the words say we 'just accept and carry on' but on the other, we are told *'we* can decide what to do with our joys and

4

griefs.' In a time of grieving, when our decision-making process is surely diminished, we have to choose to make some kind of informed decision that will embrace hope again, in order to become more familiar with the grieving, mourning process. It is very difficult to know how to make the choice, but many of us do it very quickly.

I am undoubtedly a decider. I decided very early on that I was going to confront my grief. I saw it as an adversary to be overcome, or else how could I live meaningfully?

I decided to grab grief by its lapels and shake it up. No way was it going to beat me. This brought me often to considering Elisabeth Kübler-Ross's framework for grieving, which divides the process into a linear five-point progression, through shock/denial to anger, bargaining, depression and acceptance. I learned that this framework was originally devised as a tool for those faced with, and supporting others, with terminal illness, but over time it has become known as the DABDA model of grief and loss. A Google search will reveal numerous versions and adaptations of the original premise.

I have long felt that the grieving process is nowhere near as linear as Kübler-Ross suggests – though that is not a criticism, rather it is an observation and I enjoy challenging it in my own ruminations.

And it is all very well reading about these stages in the

cold light of day when you are not living through loss, but just try being self-analytical when you are in the first throes of surviving the darkest of dark places of early grief! It is all you can do to put one foot in front of the other, let alone think about how you are coping, and which stage may reflect where you are at that moment.

I see the definitions as rather flat and one dimensional.

- Where is the rhythm that exists in the process of grief, its poetic swoops and dives, its hope, its soul, its spirit, its positivity?

- Where are all the words that are shared about the process, those hopeful and helpful descriptions that normalise our emotions as we stumble blindly along the unfamiliar road?

- Where are the signs of the upward turn that gradually comes as we emerge from the fog of shock?

- Where is the loving kindness and support that others may offer?

- Where is evidence of the reconstruction, the working through, the assimilation of this truly extraordinary thing that has happened in our lives?

- Where is the warp and weft of the fabric of grief's progression as we move forward in constructing our new normality?

- Where is the sense that often in early grief our longing

is so great that we go out looking for that person who died? We seek them in the clouds in the sky, in the whisper of the breeze, the scent of a perfume, the beauty of nature ... and when we get to a more healing place, well ... then we find them.

Our loved ones have been there all the while ... they are around us, not visible in our time now ... but nonetheless they are there. We raise our faces to the warmth of the sun, and we feel the healing process like balm to our broken heart.

- How can the spirit of these people whom we loved so much just disappear into the ether?
- Depending on our beliefs, we may be deeply comforted by those signs and symbols that are the answers to prayers and meditations in relation to those who are no longer on this plane. But it all starts with hope.

In themselves, the words of the grief model are descriptive but negative:

Shock does little towards defining that most traumatic of insults to the heart. Shock is nature's way of protecting us with a numbing of emotion so that we can begin to absorb what has happened. It dumbs us down, reduces us to beings who can only focus on our next breath, our next seconds and minutes of carrying on, and it only gradually diminishes. It is impossible to put a timescale on how long the shock of loss will last as it depends on numerous factors. I used to think that the shock of loss was greater if death came through accident. I have learned through the experience of other bereaved parents, that even when a child's death is sadly expected, through terminal illness, for example, the shock when the person dies is fundamentally the same as it is for a parent who loses a child in a sudden manner. It strikes me that there are many similarities in the shockwaves of loss but concurrent individuality in each specific case, something of a paradox.

Denial represents the mind's refusal to accept that thing which the heart already knows, and it takes a long time for the two elements of practicality and emotion to balance into being able to face the hard, cold fact of death with any kind of equanimity. As humans, we are good at denial. It is a form of self-preservation, especially early on in loss. We can quite easily pretend that our loved ones are still with us, as that is a less painful option. Personally, I don't see this as harmful. Even now, 18 years on, I can mentally conjure up my mum standing at her kitchen window and find comfort in the memory, whilst fully accepting that she is no longer here in the physical sense.

Anger is the bitter bile that can engulf us if we are not careful. How much more satisfying and helpful it is to take that anger and channel its energy into something more gainful and positive!

I remember how angry I felt when mum, who was such a kind and gentle person, fell prey to serious illness and subsequently died.

I railed at God at the time as I felt it was so unfair that a good person had been taken; I gave up in the end asking, 'Why?' and had to accept what happened to her was inevitable and I would never know the reason.

Aside from that, my anger in grief has generally been deflected into relatively harmless ire at superficial elements of my life – I can become extremely cross over the most trivial things, such as getting in the wrong supermarket queue or being tailgated on the motorway. I have come to realise that these expressions of irritation simply deflect away from the hurting anger I feel at my loss and they are blandly articulated, but somehow helpful. Deflection is another very useful technique familiar to the griever. Often when bereaved, we tend to become very busy people, filling our time in ways which take us away from the treadmill of examining grief.

Bargaining has never had much of a place in my own grief, but I understand the idea. It could be that negotiation with a higher power in exchange for nothing else bad happening may help to make us feel stronger.

Depression is truly a grey word. Clinical depression

leaches out the entire colour from our world. Grief and depression can be inextricably linked and if our domain is consistently monochrome then it may be appropriate to seek medical help. Positive thoughts and actions have a beneficial effect on feeling low, but are not in themselves sufficient to cure true depression.

Depression is a desperately miserable place, a sunken hollow that, with the help of talking therapies and/or medication, gently and gradually begins to lift into a calmer place of sad reflection. When it steadily releases its hold, we may feel that we are now at a point where we can choose to reflect on loss and although that brings sadness, it is therapeutically healing, rather than destructive.

Acceptance in loss is in part learning to accept that who we are now is not, and cannot ever be, who we were before.

BUT the upside of this is that we can arrive at this point at all, given the pain and turmoil that we have experienced. Grief is an integral part of the healing process and acceptance lies alongside healing.

Although it is a challenging idea to absorb, I believe that we need to feel the pain of grief and loss in order to measure our recovery as we look back at how it has been achieved. It is hard work and the rewards are difficult to quantify.

Instant happiness cannot be ours. An entirely carefree, untroubled existence cannot be ours again in quite the same way.

But we are still here, functioning, still standing, still full of all the emotions that make us human and indeed, probably possessing more empathy and consideration of others than we had before. These are the unanticipated gifts of loss which eventually become ours.

The stages of grief are like markers that reflect back to us and those around us, just how our mode of being and living is affected by this most profound change and shift in our being.

I invariably replace the word 'acceptance' with 'assimilation' when thinking about the loss of my son. For I do not believe that any parents can ever accept the loss of their child.

The wrongness of being predeceased by your children is absolute.

I can accept the loss of my parents, having partially worked through my grief for them, because that loss, though dreaded, was anticipated ... eventually. It is after all the natural order and they were fortunate to have lived their lives in a 'normal' timespan.

When my mother died in 2001, *I did not feel an absence of hope at the time.*

I was caught up in the process of supporting my father in

his loss. I was not hopeless, then.

When my ex-husband died suddenly in November 2002, *I did not feel an absence of hope at the time.* Rather, I felt angry then. I already mourned the loss of my marriage, now I felt the weighty responsibility of looking after our teenage children without their father's input. I did not handle this loss very well at the time. I was not experiencing an absence of hope. Rather I felt an unfair resentment at the hand life had dealt me. It took a while before I could assimilate all this and feel hopeful for a positive future again, but I never lost hope that I would recover and find the path through the obstacles before me.

Early in 2003, just a few months after the death of my ex-husband, my dad, who never recovered from the loss of my dear Mum, also passed away. I was numb with grief and I had an overwhelming desire to remove all these negative events from my life, to live 'normally' as I felt everyone else was living.

But, *I did not feel an absence of hope at the time.* Dad's death did not leave me hopeless, or helpless. It was another hurt to be borne and I worked through the practicalities once again, although I do not think I have ever truly mourned him or properly grieved for him. I read a lot about grief and loss during that period to try to make sense of all that had happened. I came to trust my instincts that the way

I was dealing with my loss was right for my particular circumstances.

Moving on a few years, my life became full of hope and optimism again, culminating in the pinnacle of my hope and happiness, my marriage to Shaun in June 2005. A scant six weeks later saw the shockingly sudden death of James. I was plunged - we all were - from the top of the world to the depths of hell. It is painful to describe the sense of despair and the true desolation that surrounded me then. James's passing was truly the worst experience of my life.

I felt an absence of hope at the time.

Hope and I had a conversation, in a place somewhere between waking and dreaming.

It was only a matter of weeks since James died and I lay in bed in the quiet of the night, the silent tears trickling from my eyes, whilst Shaun slept beside me. I lay still, not wishing to disturb Shaun and as I stared up at the ceiling, I heard a gentle, soothing voice,

"Come on," said Hope, *"Don't despair. I am here. It will get better."*

"How?" I replied, *"How am I ever going to get beyond this wrenching, despondent agony at the loss of my precious boy? How can I ever be truly happy again?"*

"With my help, you will," Hope told me. *"I will guide you towards light, faith, love and resilience. Trust in me, believe in me. I am your cornerstone,*

13

don't give up on me or you will indeed be lost."

"But surely," I argued, *"there is nothing that can make this better. To my mind, the only thing that could make it all better would be if we could turn back time and change the sequence of events so that James did not needlessly lose his life. In my heart of hearts, I know that it is not possible, but oh, how I wish it could happen."*

"I am sorry, Andrea, but the truth is that we cannot influence the past. But we can work together to influence the future. You need the will and the strength to move yourself forward, to propel yourself out of the darkness. I am here to help you gain that strength."

"OK, Hope, I hear what you say … but how do we do this?"

"If you can bring yourself to reach out towards tomorrow's dawn with even a tiny hint of optimism, that will help you. I will help you. You only have to wish for things to be better to begin to believe in the light that lies ahead, and you will start to build up the strength to work through this truly awful, dreadful period."

"Thank you, Hope," I said, before falling into a refreshing, dreamless sleep, to wake feeling marginally more positive. Once I had embraced the conceptual truth of Hope's existence, I began to see that there was indeed a path through the darkness to the light, and I started to seek out other associated elements which were ultimately to smooth my pathway, in ways I had never previously imagined. They did not arrive in any particular order, although hope was the first ingredient in the recipe which

ultimately includes light, vision, gifts, faith, love, keys and resilience, all of which bind together into a whole which has become my toolkit, my grief support system. If they were drawn into a jigsaw, the pieces would be constantly changing in size and importance but the completed whole would remain the same. The system as a whole and in its individual sections has become the rod and the staff which comfort me throughout all my days and nights.

Hope was the first signpost to place itself in the chartless desert of grief into which I was flung with James's passing. Desmond Tutu said[3], *"Hope is being able to see there is light despite all the darkness."*

At first, after James died, all I could focus on was getting through the next minute, hour, day ... with some semblance of normality. I wasn't thinking much of hope, then. Hope is perhaps best viewed as a mind-set that sits alongside optimism and positivity and these were not in evidence in the early days after James died. But gradually and by tiny degrees, I realised that I was beginning to feel little flashes of something more positive in my mind.

I couldn't put a timescale onto this. It was probably months before I really noticed anything properly. In the early months of grieving, I was simply going through the motions of everyday life with little focus.

But somewhere in the mind's recesses, running like an

unseen silent mechanism, hope was the motivator that got me out of bed in the morning.

I had to hold on to my intrinsic faith that if I persevered, things would get better, life would become easier and this enormous rock of loss would become less challenging to bear.

I began to formulate goals and targets which helped enormously, such as our successful three-year campaign with Kingston Council to install safety barriers and other measures at the riverside where James died. And of course, I wrote. Being able to express myself in writing has always been one of the greatest outlets for my emotions. It gradually became clear to me that my remit was to 'do grieving' to the best of my ability. I needed to get past my sense of injustice at the hand I felt I had been dealt through James's death to be able to see grief evolve from being my adversary to my teacher. And I began to get the urge to share my reactions and my grief behaviours with others through speaking and writing about what is still something of a taboo subject.

Why me? is a question often asked by those to whom misfortune seems to pay regular visits. Ultimately, I have taken on board that however pre-ordained they may appear to be, some events in our lives are utterly random, and I am now able to say, *Why not me?* without the sense of rancour and resentment that I felt at the outset.

This has been facilitated in part by hope. Hope has not achieved this in isolation, though. Hope is merely a facet of the whole mix of elements ranging from spirituality to faith, light, love, resilience, support... all of which will be explored in subsequent chapters to elucidate how the whole meshes together to produce a smooth working model.

Hope is both a belief and a choice. Hope is out there for the taking if we have the will to look for it, embrace it and utilise it in whatever ways bring us the comfort and strength to step forward from the darkness into the light.

Hope becomes a constant companion.

One April day we visited a lovely spring garden.

The sky was blue, the sun shone, and the plants were in full flower, the fresh brightness of the blooms and the verdant greens were a joy to the eye; indeed, to all the senses. I stood at the top of a grassy slope and looked out over the scene. I was filled with a great rush of emotion as I stood there.

I felt an underlying, deep sadness as I thought of James and how much I miss him, all these years on. But bubbling up through the sadness came a sense of positivity, sheer joy, optimism and hope for the future. As I turned to walk back along the path, a tiny white feather drifted down apparently from nowhere. It felt like an embodiment of angelic and earthly hope.

Hope from the past is evident in our lives today, too. On a visit to Wales, we walked through some ancient woodland. There were signs that there had once been a road here and we were told that the path we were following was the original access road to the village. There was a large boulder on the ground that had a natural hollow on the top. Apparently in the time of the Great Plague in the 1600s, visitors to the village had to wash their coins in the rainwater-filled hole, in the hope that they would not bring plague to the village from elsewhere in the country. What a tremendous example of hope! Whether it worked or not is of course unknown, but it exemplifies how hope can be embraced in many different ways. There are also the remains of a Roman lookout on the edge of the woodland, and touching the stones brings a sense of history along with a feeling of the hopes and fears of those who were protecting the land all that time ago. Historically, the term 'forlorn hope' became used in battles to describe the military volunteers who were brave (or perhaps foolhardy) enough to be the first wave of soldiers attacking in a siege. During the Napoleonic Wars British society was such that one way that soldiers could ensure advancement in their position in life was to volunteer for the forlorn hope.

Incredible though it may seem, the forlorn hope, even with its potential for being killed in battle, was the light that they saw in the darkness of their lives. Whilst it was likely that most members of the forlorn hope would be killed, those who survived would be assured of first pick of the spoils of war or alternatively guaranteed a promotion. There was no shortage of volunteers to become members of the forlorn hope.

Though it is impossible to imagine at first, the eventual outcome of the grieving process brings a return to joyful living again, and the re-introduction of anticipatory pleasure into our existence.

We should breathe, trust, believe, pray, hope, meditate, read, write, walk, run, cook, work, play, travel, garden, draw, colour, paint - do whatever it takes to power through the process, which has no timescale and will forever be a work in progress.

Our hope will be brave, but never forlorn.

If we grieve in a way that is bereft of hope, we cannot have any expectation that we will recover.

Hope takes centre stage at the beginning of the long dramatic play that could be called *learning to live through grief*. Hope is gradually joined by the supporting cast who all play their part in bringing optimism, positivity, support, empathy, friendship, love and ultimately a return to meaningful and purposeful living.

Once you are able to draw upon hope, whether it comes early or later in your grieving, you may, as I did, begin to reach out to find others who are living in similar situations and can therefore truly understand your loss. There are far more resources available now than there were when James died in 2005, but I am still full of gratitude for the first tentative, hopeful connections and friendships I made through the organisations The Compassionate Friends (TCF) and the Drowning Support Network (DSN.) In particular, in 2014 I met the Australian lady who had become my great virtual friend through our connection via the Drowning Support Network.

My dear Karen! – we refer to each other as our go-to person. I can go to Karen with anything I need to say, and in response she knows she can go to me too.

We have shared, and continue to share, so very much about our boys.

I have massive admiration for Karen because she successfully conquered her demons of travel - claustrophobia and fear of flying - to come all the way from Melbourne to the UK and other European countries with her husband Erik, during their sojourn in 2014.

After eight years of electronic exchanges and a few telephone calls, we finally met in the unglamorous surroundings of British Rail's Woking Station.

Karen and her husband Erik travelled to the UK via Amsterdam, and suddenly .... There they were! So many emails, so many shared confidences about our boys and how they passed. Our James and Karen and Erik's Sam - different but similar.

So much online talk about how we work through our grief and how we live, post loss. And how our other children and all our family relationships are affected by what has happened. How our hopes for our sons cannot now be realised, but how our hopes for the future are uplifted and made joyous with the arrival of our respective grandchildren. We have both been through funerals, weddings, births – over the years we have come to know each other well and we have been able to share our hopes and fears at every stage. We recognised in each other from the start that we are both proactive, hopeful grievers. During Karen and Erik's stay with us, Karen and I went to Kingston so that Karen could see James's plaque and the results of our campaign for better safety measures in the area (described in Chapter 4). Then we met with the friends with whom I originally connected via TCF. These are three dear friends who prefer not to be named. They are warm, compassionate women and we have all lost sons, each of us in different circumstances.

We have been meeting around four times a year for many years now. We are a tight group. We have never altered our dynamic. We share a lot. And…. dear Karen was brave enough to come to one of our 'ladies who do lunch' meetings. I have to say that the ladies were on their best behaviour! We shared an emotional few hours together with much laughter and a few tears. And afterwards I received the message:

"Just wanted to say how lovely it was to meet Karen, such a nice lady and very enjoyable lunch! Shame she can't fly over for all our lunches. I hope she enjoys her time over here, say hello from me next time you speak, or should that be 'Good Day, Sheila'….."

Together, we friends, who were drawn together by shared tragedy, represent a collective, collaborative hope. One of our original group of four has now moved away and the three of us continue to meet and develop in the commonality of our unique bond.

After their stay with us, Karen and Erik met in Gloucestershire with another mutual friend of ours, via DSN – whom I have also met twice.

A brave lady, who says:

"I had the most extraordinary time with Karen and Erik yesterday. We clicked immediately and talked nonstop about our boys, exactly how we all dealt with their deaths and how we feel about and deal with life now. It was so lovely to talk to people who understand about what we went/go

through. They are such lovely, open people and I wish I had friends like that here. It's quite strange how you can suddenly almost slot into a relationship with sombody, bonded immediately by this tragedy."

Then Karen and Erik travelled further up country. They met with DSN people whom I do not know, but they do. Then they met in Scotland with a lady who found me, my book and DSN online all at the same time. She is the lovely, warm Jackie whom I have yet to meet.

She said: *"Karen and I met up last night for drinks and a meal along with Erik and Ally. It was lovely to meet up with them, the connections between us all made for very relaxed and comfortable conversation (if a bit tearful). We talked a lot of our precious boys and also how I found DSN through reading 'Into the Mourning Light.' For me it is really lovely to hear that eventually there will be happy times ...that we will find a way of living along with the overwhelming sadness we feel."*

These friendships exemplify hope in a very special way. When I look back down the years, hope stands out as an innate strength that we all share, even if we do not entirely realise how powerful it is. The disorientation of grief needs anchoring by something palpable, strong and supportive. This is hope, often personified with an anchor, which is a universal symbol for hope. The truly extraordinary experience of grief needs normalising and grounding by an element which can be shared. This too is hope.

Hope is a word with many descriptors. It can be faint, high, unrealistic, borrowed, fond, fervent … but the hope that I believe best reflects proceeding from the darkness of grief back into the light, is a mature hope.

This is an expectant hope, a hope that is patient and steadfast despite the obstacles along the way. Mature hope is a hope that doesn't falter or give up, it runs in the background all the time the other factors in life ebb and flow as they will. It is worth remembering that as we grieve, we are also attempting to live the rest of our lives in as normal a way as possible. This has to be accompanied by the steadiness of underlying hope, otherwise we cannot succeed.

I was intrigued to learn recently that the French language contains two words to describe hope. One is in current use and that is *espoir*. *Espoir* describes everyday commonplace hopes, such as "*I hope the sun will shine today,*" whilst the other archaic word for hope, *esperance,* describes a higher order of hope; a hope that has been tested by adversity. The bereaved can favour the use of *esperance* rather than the order of *espoir,* I feel.

When I write in an email "*I hope this finds you well*" this is not simply a vain hope. It is heartfelt because I believe that we, who have experienced the depths of despair in grief, perhaps possess a different understanding of the

24

importance of hope in our lives. Without hope, we cannot move on to see the chinks of light that appear as surely as dawn follows night. Eventually we will be surrounded by and supported in the light, but there is much to work through before we arrive at that point. Hope and light are inextricably linked.

We should confidently walk into hope's outstretched arms with a sense of relief that we are being nurtured. We can stand in hope's soft light and know that she is revealing to us the first glimmers that begin to break up the darkness.

Chapter 2
Finding the Mourning Light

Dare to reach out your hand into the darkness, to pull another hand into the light.

Norman B Rice

By its very nature, the mourning light can never be exactly the same as the light that you knew and accepted in your life before loss. However hard you work at recovering the light, it will always have a slightly reduced lucidity and brightness.

Where does the light start? In essence, light is as essential to you and me as breathing, water, bread and salt. There is much debate about how your inner light can shine again after you have been summarily plunged into darkness.

The light of transformation after loss begins with hope and the intention to move forward, even though your fear of the new unknown is great.

Perhaps the key to rekindling your light is to actively seek out ways that you can make it shine. By lighting your own path, you also light the way for others who are struggling to find their light.

The message attributed to Hermes, messenger of the Gods says[1], "*as above, so below, as within, so without, as the universe, so is the soul.*" This principle of reflective correspondence is good to learn in relation to darkness and light. I take it to mean that the likeness of your own state, whether it is dark or light, is that which is picked up by others and mirrored back to you. It is easy to prove this if you experiment with smiling at strangers. If you present as open, cheerful and friendly in your dealings with people, whether or not you know them, this is indeed reflected back to you. However, it is a tall order in the early days of grieving and I believe that you need periods of introspection and visits to the darker places to be able to assess progress, as you emerge into the mourning light and appreciate all that it has to offer.

The rewards are worth the journey. Once you have experienced the acute contrast between grief's darkness and the light, you begin to understand how your attitude of mind can alter how you perceive both. It is simplistic to say that if you wish to change something in your life you need only to alter your inner attitude to it, but there is a grain of truth in that, and if you start by having an aspiration to see things differently, this is the first step to achieving true change.

The mourning light has the ability to grow and increase, the more you embrace it.

In other words, once you are able to live with a modicum

of joy again, your happiness infects others and you realise that you are back in the mainstream of life. The good news is that the light intensifies over time and you can see its gathering brilliance when you look back and see how far you have come. You emerge into the light, not by denying your pain, but by walking through and working through it.

When we visited Turkey on holiday, we stayed in a hotel near the river. Early in the morning the water was crystal clear, and we walked through beautiful gardens to the hotel jetty to watch the fish and the terrapins that are indigenous to the area. Shoals of tiny fry glittered and sparkled just under the sunlit surface, and the water reflected the light like glass. Later in the day, after numerous boats had been plying up and down the channel, the water became pellucid, its milky green depths still beautiful but opalescent. It had lost the sharp clarity of the morning. We could glimpse the piscine life beneath the surface, but it was softer, more indistinct, though retaining its form.

So it is with the mourning light.

Sometimes, when I feel particularly happy, the mourning light shimmers with a radiance I recognise but it does not throw life's landscape into sharp relief in quite the same way as I perceived light before. There is an adjustment, a toning down, an unquantifiable reduction in the strength of the light. But it is still light! There is a shadow behind it, therefore it is a light. And you grow to accept it as your norm. The photographer's eye assesses three attributes of light: intensity, quality and direction. Each of these is a variable, and you too learn these variables as you process how you are living in the mourning light. Like adjusting to new spectacle lenses, learning to be in the mourning light requires you to make small changes to how you interpret everything you experience, with each of your senses.

The sudden traumatic loss of someone you love, be it parent, partner, friend or child brings darkness crashing in; the blackest, darkest, deepest, dark you can imagine. It feels like the loneliest place on earth, yet you need to be able to believe you are not alone in the darkness in order to be able to begin to embrace the light.

You have to calm yourself sufficiently to be in the blackness without trying to fight it, in order for it to begin to show you what you can achieve.

You have to sit in the darkness, learn not to be afraid of it, and discover how it can be your ally in giving you the strength from the ashes of your despair.

You have to learn not to succumb to the fear that will destroy your ability to find the light. Confront that fear, banish the terror that threatens to swamp you and out of the grey mists of your tangled thoughts will come the clarity of the dawning, mourning light.

Then you are able to reach out tentatively to the brilliance that lies on the obverse side of the coin of the dark.

I am invariably reminded of the grim days of early grief during the short days of winter, when we go to work in the dark, or just when the late dawn breaks, and we return home when it is already nightfall. In the early days after James died, I was often awake in the deepest hours and in some respects the night's embrace was a comforting cocoon. I did not have to face anyone else, and I could give vent to my grief privately, which has always been my preferred way.

I am not great at public weeping. How I envy those people who can weep elegantly with unchanged features, not like I do, ending up with red puffy eyes and a blocked nose!

Whether you analogise your grief as a pit, hole, cave, void, chasm – whatever it is, you can take comfort that with your innate strength and determination the light can, and will, return.

Do not despair that the darkness of grief will overwhelm you. You must work through the darkness to emerge into the mourning light, and it **will** happen, just as surely as day follows night.

Sometimes, you have to be in the darkest place possible to realise that you are at the nadir. The extreme limitation of being in that place can release far more potential than you realise.

The knowledge that, in early loss, you really cannot feel any worse, might be the springboard that turns you towards the mourning light. Finding sources of light begins to dispel the darkness. At first, it may be very small, simple things that lift your spirits. A thoughtful card from a friend, a particularly enjoyable meal, a favourite walk … all these things begin to penetrate the grey, dark moments and become welcome as time passes. The empathy of others and the connections that you start to make as you emerge from the darkest point of your grief are often the first lights that soften your grief and you can begin the true healing process.

One of the most important ways I began to embrace the emergence of my mourning light was to seek out uplifting sustenance for my poor, bruised and battered spirit. I have written before of the path that took me from a visit to a Mind, Body and Spirit show to the Harry Edwards Healing Sanctuary in Shere, where on an Open Day I serendipitously bumped into my friend and fellow bereaved parent Linda Sewell. The Sanctuary is in the most apposite location for uplifting the soul and spirit and a visit there is highly recommended, whether you have any faith, or none.

Linda's grief path since her son Tom died in 2008 has led her to becoming a spiritual healer. She has also trained as a non-denominational Celebrant, offering an excellent, individually tailored, bespoke service for weddings, funerals, renewal of vows, and any other ceremony requiring the services of a personal celebrant.

We have co-presented two bereavement workshops, in 2014 and 2015.

One day in the late summer of 2013, as we sat enjoying the afternoon sun at the Sanctuary, Linda said,

"Wouldn't this be a lovely place to hold a workshop for bereaved parents? The surroundings and the energies are ideal."

"Yes," I replied, and thought no more of it.

A week or so later, an email from Linda popped into my inbox. *"Do you remember I mentioned the thought of a workshop?"* she said, *"I've floated the idea with a few people at the Sanctuary and they agree it would be welcome. How would you feel about co-presenting it with me?"*

I shared Linda's feeling that we were well suited to do this and readily agreed. We met again and our excitement grew as we began to formulate the agenda for the day. Very early on we agreed that we wanted to convey a message of hope for our attendees, with the promise that it is possible to move forward from the dark pit of despair of early grief towards a return to living in the light.

Our theme of "The Heart's Journey" was clearly presented

to us.

By November we had the blessing of the Trustees and a date was put into the diary; Sunday 13 April 2014.

Linda has made many friends and contacts through her involvement with the Sanctuary and she invited two other bereaved parents to co-present with us, both named Lucy as it happens, as well as our willing helpers for the day: these were healers who volunteered to help us and be there to support our attendees with compassion, empathy and tissues, as required.

We wished to incorporate meditation into our programme and were delighted when Toni Jode, a lovely lady who was at that time a healer at the Sanctuary, agreed to provide this for us. Sadly, Toni passed away in 2017 after being diagnosed with and treated for a brain tumour; it is a measure of her great generosity of spirit that she was prepared to be involved with our workshop, despite having had major surgery and treatment for her illness.

Once we had the basics of our programme mapped out, we advertised the Workshop on the Sanctuary and The Compassionate Friends websites and before long we had reached our agreed capacity of 15 attendees. It is a sad fact that we could have filled the workshop twice over.

Our roles for the day became clear-cut and in a sense were a reflection of us as individuals. Linda's close links with the Sanctuary ensured plenty of support, seen and unseen. She also developed a knack for finding heart-related items in the shops! One Lucy is a teacher and artist. Her late son Oscar's friends created a music CD in his memory, the proceeds of which support a child in Haiti through sponsorship. Lucy created a beautifully designed Tree of Hearts from willow for our day and provided the art materials for the attendees to decorate it.

Our other Lucy brought her campaigning voice to the day as she was petitioning for a change in the law to allow bereaved parents paid leave from work. In her own case, following the loss of her 23-month-old son Jack to a tragic drowning accident, her partner was given just three days leave from work.

As Lucy says, *"Why should parents get maternity and paternity leave when a child is born, but next to nothing when their child passes away?"* Lucy continues to petition and campaign for this issue that is so dear to her heart.

My role was to take on the practical organisation of the day, as this is definitely within my comfort zone.

My verbal presentation would follow a similar pattern to Linda's in describing and explaining the toolbox that I have gathered about me to help work through my grief, including the cathartic process of writing. I also wanted to share what I have learned about moving into, recognising,

35

embracing and exploring the mourning light.

After a number of briefings and some fine tuning of our programme, we agreed our set up for the day, which was to provide a welcoming, caring and colourful environment for our attendees. The room we used was light and airy and we populated a resource table with appropriately themed books and items that we felt would be of interest. Sunday 13 April dawned; it was a gorgeous, clear spring day. As I drove through the entrance to the Sanctuary I felt incredibly moved by the beauty of the morning. The bluebells were just coming into flower and there was a sense of peace and loving energy pervading the whole area.

Our 15 attendees, including two couples, gradually arrived. They were initially apprehensive, but the surroundings worked their magic and our band of helpers soon put everyone at ease.

The morning programme consisted of introductions and sharing of our personal stories. The weight of grief and sadness in the room was palpable after we had all shared the facts of the loss of our beloved children. The support between all of us was immeasurable, due to the simple fact that we each understand what it is to lose a child. Naturally many tears were shed, but there was a collective compassion and empathy. We felt we were in a safe space

36

to share our emotions freely and from the heart.

To restore our equilibrium, we were indeed glad of the gentle and uplifting energy of Toni's lovely meditation, which felt very calming.

After lunch, we enjoyed a creative session which comprised of decorating hearts to put onto our tree.

A great deal of thought went into how these would be prepared, everyone seemed to enjoy the artistic expression. If they wished, the men who were present could paint a business card shape as an alternative to a heart.

One activity I particularly enjoyed was plaiting coloured embroidery silks to make a hanging loop for the heart. This necessitated working with another person to hold the thread taut and led to some lively conversation around the room.

Then we all walked and talked in the sunshine, through the beautiful grounds of the Sanctuary, before making our way back to the chapel.

There we placed the decorated hearts dedicated to our children onto the tree and Toni led us in our second prayerful meditation, which was perfectly tailored to our needs.

At the end, we each spoke our children's names into the space of the chapel, it was very moving and special to connect with them in this way.

We returned upstairs for a final share before our attendees left with keepsakes of the day which Linda had sourced, together with an attendance certificate.

Linda and I were delighted that from the seed of an idea we were able, with the help of others, to develop and grow something that flourished into a helpful, positive and uplifting day for all.

Our second workshop took place exactly a year later, with the theme of colour.

This time our programme was built around the use of colour in healing grief, and together with our artistically creative presenter Lucy, we planned a programme that would provide an uplifting and ultimately beneficial day for our attendees.

Some of our attendees had lost children in very recent times. Over the course of the morning we brought each of our children into the room with words, tears, anecdotes, photographs and even some laughter as we shared our stories.

We talked of individual tools for managing our grief, such as creativity, sport, spiritual learning, reading, writing .... Whatever works for each of us.

We shared our feelings around our children's peers and siblings and the wider family, and how we can manage all the differing emotions and reactions that we encounter.

We discussed the need to find things that rest our mind from the pain that is always there.

We emphasised the importance of finding our way out of the grey fog of early, monochrome grief, back into the light and colourful world again, to ultimately sustain us and lift our spirits.

We spoke of the use of social media to keep the memories of our children alive.

We managed to laugh at how our children would view their 'ancient' parents keeping abreast of Facebook and Twitter, but we agreed that these media provide a platform for communication, in particular with our children's friends, who most definitely do not forget them. And in turn we feel that it is a way to keep a current link with our children. Those of us who lost a child to an accident spoke of our immense and traumatic shock at having a child 'here one minute and gone the next.' It was very interesting to hear the viewpoint of one of our attendees who recently lost her son to cancer, who said:

"The devastating shock of my loss is no different to yours. Even though it was clinically spelled out to me that he would die, I still expected, prayed for and anticipated the miracle that would keep my son alive. My shock was as great as it is for those parents faced with the sudden arrival of the policeman at the door - and what that signifies."

I have long believed that every parent who suffers the

loss of a child suffers a degree of post-traumatic stress disorder. After all, what can possibly be more traumatic than the loss of a child, however it happens?

But this attendee's words certainly brought (to me at any rate) a new realisation of the impact of grief - regardless of the circumstances.

We spent a while making the most of the freedom to discuss our children without constraint, in a safe and supportive environment. (This is something that bereaved parents will recognise as rare; almost invariably those close to us inadvertently place constraints on conversations for fear of causing further distress.)

The afternoon gave us the opportunity to be mindfully creative in colouring in a mandala (a symmetrical design bounded by a circle).

We spent time together in the Sanctuary chapel to end the day and I believe from the feedback received after both workshops, that we all benefited from being in a mutually uplifting environment.

Light is crucial to our wellbeing. The disorientation of grief plunges you into a darkness that feels suffocating, often crushing. It is a kind of limbo, a liminal space which becomes the framework for the reconstruction of your life that has been shattered. You are in the most difficult of transitional states: you cannot go back to 'before', but you are not yet ready to join 'after' either.

If it is true that your inner light is not extinguished all the time you draw breath and beyond, then you have to search for it in the depths of your loss and sadness. You may be able to restore it through faith, hope and the support of others; often it is a combination of factors that contribute, much like the process of grieving itself.

Just as the sun hides behind the clouds, yet you know it is still there; so it is with your own light. I remember when a friend of mine travelled on a plane for the first time. She told me she was surprised that once the aircraft was above the cloud layer, there was constant brilliant sunshine, and she had never known it would be like that. This sounds pleasingly naïve but in fact it is easy to think, when you are in the depths of mourning, that the sun has disappeared behind the clouds forever.

Mourning is grief in action. It is not passive; this is one of the reasons why it feels like such very hard work.

One of the chief functions of effective grieving and mourning is to be able to turn on your own light again and see that lightness radiate back out from your own personal world. Mourning 'successfully' allows you to feel a deep connection with those whom you have lost, and hold close their memory, while also being able to move forward into a meaningful future without them.

It is true to say that there is no right or wrong way to grieve. I have said before that how we mourn, how we process our individual loss, is an entirely personal journey. The best we can hope for when we are in the darkest recesses of early loss is the pointers along the way which inch us forward back into a semblance of living in the light. Eventually, loss is integrated into our past rather than being brought into our future.

Often the saddest part of grieving is thinking not so much of what you will miss without your loved one, but of all the things he or she will miss by not being here anymore: such as the family weddings, births, parties, celebrations … But sadness is an essential part of processing what has happened. I believe you need to experience the symptoms of grief to begin to normalise the process of mourning in your own mind. I remember a phase of feeling particularly lethargic and I discovered that this is described as anhedonia, particularly in relation to grieving, meaning 'an inability to experience pleasure in activities which were formerly pleasurable.'

The listlessness of this phase was not the same as a deep depression; rather it was an 'I can't be bothered' period. Paradoxically, being in such a stultified state seemed to allow me to have sufficient stillness in my mind to connect with the darkness, and almost to welcome its blanket effect.

I needed the withdrawal that the lethargy provided at the time. I had to embrace all the emotions I felt, whether they were good or bad, in order to learn from each thing that was happening. I had to experience the shattering reality before I could re-emerge with any of the elements of positive transformation that were provided by the mourning light.

Wouldn't it be lovely if, after a given time, be it a year, two years, five or ten, we suddenly woke up one morning feeling we were utterly 'cured' from grieving? Straight and tall we would stand, ready to walk out into the bright sunlight of normality again.

But actually … would it be so lovely?

We need the balance of opposites to understand the highs and lows. Nowhere is this more evident than in grief. The pain is offset by the relief, when grief lessens. The darkness is offset by the light. We need the sorrow to be able to embrace the joy.

Whatever our goals in life, they generally take time, effort and not a little hardship to achieve. Take study, for example. Any worthwhile academic or educational course calls for a level of application and commitment, first of all to learn the basic principles and then to apply the principles in an increasingly advanced and informed way until we reach the fulfilment of attaining the qualification or passing the required grades to move on to the next level.

Whilst study is generally linear, mourning is not.

If there was a qualification in grieving, the course would be long and arduous, the tests would contain a great deal of self-examination and reflective practice. It would be impossible to state who would be best qualified to teach such a course, but there is no way it would be any good at all if the leaders and tutors were not themselves experienced in working through grief from the darkness back into the light.

One of the greatest problems with the hypothetical grief course would be setting the syllabus, because each student's path would be entirely individual and unique, thus making it impossible to standardise. There, are, however, several givens in grief that we can all consider as they reflect the commonality of bereavement, loss and mourning:

- It is the hardest thing you do in your life
- You have to work at it constantly
- You will emerge from the darkness into the light eventually, however you approach your grief path.

On the face of it, you may wonder, *"why bother?"*

For me there was no question after James died but to work as diligently as possible, as I felt a strong desire not to let down my new husband and family. I appreciate that not everyone has others around them to consider and that must make it even more difficult, but it is ultimately rewarding to persevere, even if the only person measuring your progress is yourself.

I also felt that if I gave in, grief would win, and I would be letting down James's memory. He knew me as a strong person, and somehow, I had to hold onto that strength, harness it with whatever means I had at my disposal, and soldier on.

I have adopted a multi-pronged approach that sees me reaching out in many directions, individually and simultaneously. I take a bit from here, a bit from there, and mesh it all together until eventually I arrive at some sort of cohesive process that moves me forward.

It is worth remembering that darkness and light are duality rather than opposing forces. Nothing is purely dark or purely light in reality. In grief terms, it is difficult to describe the mourning light as an entity in itself.

Perhaps it is best considered as that which is achieved through the emotions and thoughts that you want the most, such as gratitude for the life that was lived, the happiness brought by it and the love that remains, though the physical person has gone.

There are many representations of light which are

comforting and uplifting. Perhaps the simplest and most symbolic is a candle. Universally accepted, it ranges from a tea light in the home to a pillar candle in a place of worship, from an Olympic torch to a beacon on the hillside.

Every second Sunday in December sees the annual candle-lighting ceremony organised by The Compassionate Friends. TCF is an international organisation, hence the candle-lighting takes place at 7pm local time across the globe. What a wonderful concept! - as each time zone arrives at 7pm, a wave of light is sent up to the heavens on behalf of our children. Wherever they may be, they will be able to see it.

This ritual of lighting a candle on a specific day at a particular time and being part of a collective rite that asks so little but gives so much is somehow very comforting to those in grief. If you are not grieving, you can light a candle for someone who is, and that small altruistic act brings a sense of empathy.

Today, I lit a candle. I watched the alchemy as I held the match to the wick. With a tiny miracle, the flame leapt; a living brightness in front of me. What would the candle flame say to me if it could speak? What thoughts might be in the little powerhouse contained in the living flame? …
I imagined it could say:

"I am your light. I am your illumination. I am spiritual, divine, and intelligent. I know when you need me. I am your hope in the night, your avenger against the darkness. I represent those whom you honour.

I warm you; I embrace you; I uplift you, I help you. I remember.

Seek me out as you seek out hope.

I am always at your fingertips. I am synonymous with faith, love, peace, joy and resilience. Look for me, even in places where you would not expect to find me.

I light the darkest of your thoughts, I am the radiance of your heart.

I live inside your soul. I am in your mind always.

You can depend on me to light your path wherever it takes you.

Whenever and wherever you light a candle, I connect with your soul and your spirit. I symbolise all the love that you give and all the love that you receive.

When you were born, I lit you from within, even before you took your first breath. And do not imagine that I will leave you with your last breath, for then you will pass into the lightest, brightest light of all."

I write often of the premise that the darkness of grief eventually gives way to being able to live life in the light again and the symbolism of each individual candle, bringing its own light, underlines this. Even after the blackest, darkest of dark nights, a new day will invariably dawn.

Your capacity for embracing the positive is outweighed in early grief but it is reclaimable.

I think you have as much to learn from embracing the

47

darkness as you have from welcoming in the light. Recognising that loss can give you opportunities to blossom and grow is a difficult concept, but suffering can indeed be a positive tool for transformation and growth. In the end, you can choose to walk forward into the mourning light rather than remain sitting in the dark. You may trust light without question, because it is on the face of it entirely positive. You need to learn to trust the darkness in a similar way.

I read a fictional concept that a child believed that if you let darkness into a well-lit room, it would become dark, just as it becomes light in the morning when you let in the light.

It is a logical enough notion. The darkness of grief eclipses all the light of your life, but the trick is to learn how not to be subsumed by it. You have to find ways to pull back the curtains, push up the blinds and let the light back in again. I would love to be able to say that being in the mourning light is wholly positive; after all, it is the reverse of the darkness. However, it is fair to say that in early grief at least, you may feel that you are constantly in the unwelcome glare of a spotlight, well before you are ready to step out from the wings.

Centre stage you stand, emotionally bare and vulnerable whilst all around you people look at you with pity, saying, *"ahh, poor soul.   He/she has lost their loved one … how hard it must be …"*

These are the times when you feel your raw helpless state is everyone else's prerogative and even property on which to observe, question, judge and have an opinion.

Whilst sympathy is undoubtedly well meant, it is not helpful to you when you do not have the strength to be responsive or reactive to the opinions and thoughts of others.

These are the times when it may indeed be comforting to wrap yourself in the warm darkness, holding close the knowledge that you do not need to justify yourself, answer questions about how you feel or feel pressured into presenting yourself in any semblance of your normal form … until the day comes that you are ready to do so.

How you behave in grief should be both forgiving and if necessary, forgiven by others around you.   There are acceptable reactive norms of grief behaviour which are well recognised but they may shock those around you. For example, a dark sense of humour may be a coping strategy for you which can shock others.

In your emotionally raw state, you may be intolerant of others, or conversely you may say *"yes"* to everything and find yourself totally overwhelmed with commitments that you then have to cancel because you cannot face them.

49

It always makes me feel (grimly) amused when I hear of people asking the relatively recently bereaved, *"Are you feeling better?"* as if they have been suffering with the flu.

'Feeling better' is an alien concept to begin with, in grief. It has no place within the struggle to overcome the darkness and begin to re-establish your place in the light in which everyone else appears to be living. Nothing that you do, whether it is negative or positive can alter the reality of the finality of death.

Looking for the positive and seeking out light in the darkness is a more constructive use of your energy which, to begin with, would far rather channel itself into fury and resentment. Recognising the simple fact that you have to survive your trauma to be able to live meaningfully again is often the first step towards the mourning light.

Sunlight is essential to our wellbeing. Everyone smiles more when it is sunny. Do you prefer the early days of summer, when the leaves on the trees are fresh and green and there is still a slight cool edge to the air? Or do you crave the mellow warmth of the late summer sun that sheds soft shadows and caresses warm skin like balm? The mourning light has more of the attributes of that softer, later season sunshine, to my mind. And who can resist a crisp, frosty winter's morning when the lemon-yellow sun lights nature's magic on the grass and plants?

Sunlight is indeed a life-giver to all of nature's wonders and it is an essential feature in our lives. I remember feeling very resentful that the sun carried on shining after James died. My mood cried out for the mad energy of storms and shrieking winds. But the world turned on its axis regardless, and the balmy summer days continued unabated.

The relative predictability of the weather can be both a boon and a curse.

The moon, too, is a comforting symbol of steadfast light. It changes frequently, just as you and I do. Every day it's a different version of itself, and there is comfort in its cycles of waxing and waning.

I love that the moon exerts such a subtle influence on us – particularly for women whose own cycles are affected by the phases of the moon. Sometimes the moon is weak and pale, sometimes it is full of strong, clear, directional light. It reveals itself as a crescent with much hidden, or a full and open face. As it is with the mourning light.

Light and joy are synonymous, as are darkness and despair. But if you have known light and joy, you can recapture both. Elisabeth Kübler Ross said[2]:

"People are like stained-glass windows. They sparkle and shine when the sun is out, but when the darkness sets in, their true beauty is revealed only if

there is a light from within."

There are myriad facets to the light within. It is never truly extinguished, and I would ascribe to it a mercurial personality. If hope is the bedrock of your life, then light is the herald that guides your way. When I think of James, it seems that his life light was snuffed out too soon and too fast. Yet the light that he shone on the world remains in my mind and heart. Perhaps it is his soul light that continues to uplift and encourage me even through my darkest moments. Similarly, my mother beamed a soft, kindly light on others throughout her life. Her soul light also resides in my heart.

Even when your loved ones are gone, the mourning light reinforces your faith that they remain with you, lighting your way.

Once you embrace the mourning light, you are ready to begin to give voice to how you feel, to be able to articulate for the benefit of others, how you are coping and moving forward despite your loss. Moving into the arena of helping others seems to be a goal of many of those who have lost loved ones. Hope and the mourning light are a powerful combination that begins this work which is likely to remain in progress for the rest of your days.

If you can take up the torch offered by the mourning

light and shine it outwards, then you are indeed impelling yourself out of the depths of your grief into a better place.

The Light of Hope and Mourning

The candle is lit; see the light
Soft at first, then glowing bright
Like a beacon in the night
Bringing you to our mind's sight

Clever match with tiny spark
Dispels the fears held in the dark
On memory's journey we can embark
Recalling how you left your mark

The flame burns strong and tall and true
Spirited; reminding us of you
How wonderfully through our lives you blew
Our pride and hope and love you drew
And if in sadness, our tears should flow
There is comfort in the candle's glow
Solace and healing may be slow
But gradual joy we come to know

We breathe in light in this special space
And feel soothed as darkness is displaced
Your love we hold close, never to replace
It stays as dear as your smiling face

The candle is lit; see the light shine
The flame is upright and clear and fine
A symbol of peace; across the world we align
United in loss, be it yours or mine.

Andrea Corrie   November 2017

Chapter 3
Proceeding Through Grief

'Our children do not die. They live on in our hearts with wingbeats of memory.'
Andrea Corrie

When we reached 28 July 2015, the anniversary marking a decade of loss, I wrote about how our world changed forever ten years before.

The greatest fear of any parent became our reality. James went out for the evening and he never returned. He was not found for three days, after which he was recovered from the River Thames at Kingston, his death by drowning a tragic accident.

I cannot easily bring myself to write the words *his body was recovered* because that does not convey the depth of feeling surrounding the loss of the wonderful, individual being who was James: that handsome, bright, funny, vibrant, cheeky, boy; on the threshold of manhood, his future so full of promise. He was snatched from his life and all our lives, in an instant.

And there we were.

Suddenly it seemed, the calendar told us we were ten years on.

Battered, bruised but still standing.

Over the decade, I amassed an amazing amount of useful first-hand knowledge of grief and the grieving process, primarily as it applies to my own situation.

Certain aspects of grief are common to all types of loss, but other features are entirely specific to child loss.

I have become a reluctant expert, first learning how to deal with my own feelings and then gradually grasping an appreciation of how my loss affects others in the wider circle. Sharing my thoughts and emotions in writing is undoubtedly cathartic. It helps me to break down the enormity of loss into more palatable bite-size pieces.

I have watched a clip on YouTube called 'Put the Glass down: How long to hold on to grudges and trauma'[1]

Paraphrased, it goes something like this:

A professor holds up a glass half full of water to his students, asking,

"How much does this weigh?"

The students guess at the weight. Prof says,

"Really my question is not so much how much it weighs, but what would happen if I held it up for some minutes … or an hour … or a day?"

The students' reply was that sooner or later, he would have arm ache and muscle stress and the pain would become intolerable.

"Does the weight of the glass change?" asked the professor.

"*No,*" came the answer.

"*So, what causes the arm ache and muscle stress? What should I do to come out of pain?*"

The answer is, of course, to *put the glass down.*

You need to put your 'glass of grief' down for relief. I have learned that both holding and putting down are possible, individually and concurrently. It's a real mix.

The toxicity of holding on to negative emotions which are detrimental to the psyche is, I think, an important feature to consider. The longer you hold on to the worst aspects of loss, the greater is your pain, and you may find yourself paralysed by it. Mulling over the most awful features of loss and learning the techniques that allow you to put these down at will, can help bring perspective to the process.

For myself, the only way to minimise the destructive elements of the trauma and grief I have experienced is to gradually examine and work through them at my own pace and in my own way.

The learning curve is steep, and signposts are helpful, but it is inbuilt strength and resilience that win through in the end.

I will always wish I could take away the pain of the loss of James, not just from myself but from the rest of the family, his friends, and all the people who knew him. Grief is indeed a heavy burden and the process of lightening it takes a long time. We all carry it in different ways and wish we could turn the clock back. The only aspect of acceptance in grief that I embrace is that it is, sadly, impossible to undo the events of the past.

Where did I stand at the close of ten years of loss?

I can truthfully say I had integrated the loss of James into my life to a comfortable level, where I was able to stand back and look down the years with the satisfaction of knowing I have achieved significant steady progress along the way.

If you are analytical by nature, as I am, you may well find yourself challenging the commonly laid down grief stages which tend to favour a linear, progressive approach. These do not, for me, reflect the 'two steps forward, one back' nature of my path as I am living it. My attention has been drawn to the 1995 paper by Margaret Stroebe and Henk Schut, rather wordily called 'The Dual Process Model of Coping with Bereavement.'[2] This theorises that if you are working through your grief, i.e. tackling it head on, you must also give yourself time off from the process in order to give yourself a break and to be able to move forward to the next stage in the assimilation procedure. This type of theorising resonates well with me. I tend to work on a chore and reward system, in any case. For example, my reward after the chore of cleaning the kitchen will be to watch some mindless TV, read a book or check my emails. I think a chore and reward system can equally be applied to grieving.

The inevitable chore of opening the box of your difficult emotions, taking them out, examining them, putting them away again, will necessarily leave you feeling tired, sad and empty.

So, reward yourself with some leisure time; go for a run, bake a cake, do something creative; whatever makes you feel positive and happy again. This cycle undoubtedly becomes easier with repetition. Embracing a positive mind-set, knowing that at the end of the difficult task you will be doing something to make yourself feel better, seems to work well psychologically.

I like too Stroebe and Schut's discussion around two types of stressors associated with grieving: *loss orientation* and *restoration orientation*. Both types require coping mechanisms, and breaks are also important.

Stroebe and Schut define loss orientation as emotion-focused coping and processing loss, whilst restoration-oriented stressors relate more to having to compensate for the person who is no longer here.

This may be more relevant to losing a spouse/sibling than a child, I feel, because the focus is on external adjustments following loss (for example, if your husband always looked after the household accounts, now you have to learn to do so). It is still an important concept to consider when thinking about what constitutes progress in your grief.

Losing a child puts a burden on a parent to somehow be more than they were before.

There is a need to fill the child-shaped hole with something that comes from within. It is a difficult concept. I often feel I am trying hard to compensate for James no longer being here – and that is achieved by pushing myself further than I would have done before, right across the board. Time has become infinitely more precious, and I do not like to waste my days. I feel a need to keep driving myself forward and I recognise this as a coping mechanism.

There is no doubt that Stroebe and Schut have it right when they suggest that we oscillate between confrontation and avoidance in processing loss. It is vital to do whichever feels right at the time. Avoidance or diversion gives the mind necessary breaks from the hard work and application that is required in grieving.

I have noticed that most of the bereaved parents I meet are invariably very busy people, and in part this perhaps reflects our desire to fill our time with compensatory items to divert us from pain. This is not to deride our busyness, which is also very useful and productive.

All this is a somewhat dry theoretical discussion on what

is actually my day to day living process. What has it to do with my traversing the rocky road of grief for the loss of James?

I can illustrate my progress over the past decade by singling out a 'top ten' of useful things I have learned, inasmuch as they relate generally and also more specifically to my own situation. I hope others are able to apply them and be helped by the ideas and suggestions tailored to their own needs.

1   **Gathering a support network around you really helps**

You may not be a 'group person' or a joiner – but there is plenty of available help for the bereaved. You can do as much or as little as you like in terms of seeking out support.

The isolation of early grief leaves you fragile, vulnerable and lacking in confidence and often the first step in contacting a group is very hard, but ultimately worthwhile.

You may find that sharing your experiences or being aware of others going through similar circumstances is immensely helpful. You may find newfound confidence – not in comparing your grief, which should never be competitive, but in realising that you are coping in the best way possible **for yourself**.

Grief is necessarily individual and self-absorbed,

particularly in the early days, for you are compelled to constantly review how you are coping, what you are managing, etc, etc. Your family and friends are naturally your main support, but it is sometimes difficult to share your grief path with them, this is where outside support can be useful. You can feel that you are adding to the burden of other family members' sense of loss by sharing your own and this heaps on the guilt that you may feel.

It is difficult **not** to feel you have to be strong for everyone else around you, but initially at least, you must centre in on yourself to cope with the maelstrom of emotion to which you have to adjust. You are not only coping with new feelings but also likely to be dealing with the practicalities and officialdom surrounding a loss, which is daunting in itself. Joining The Compassionate Friends and the Drowning Support Network helped me because each resource provided a forum where I found empathy, understanding and support in equal measures. It is entirely true to say that no one else can truly understand what you are going through unless they have suffered similar loss. Knowing that others had gone through all the protocols and processes involved in the aftermath of death helped a little in minimising the hurdles that must be overcome.

2   **Find faith that it will get better**

In early grief, you are likely to feel cast adrift in a new, dark world that does not come with a map. The darkness of the pit, black hole, cave, is absolute at first. An immense amount of personal strength and resilience is required for you to begin to approach the chinks of light which gradually appear. Embrace them.

I vividly remember contacting my TCF personal mentor very early on and asking him, *"Will I always feel as dreadful as this?"* and his reply,

"No, Andrea, you will gradually feel better as time passes." I envied him his stance of being 12 years along the line at the time and tried to believe his words; indeed, I clung to them to give me hope for the future.

At the beginning, I often sought out models of people who were moving forward positively and coping with grief and loss, in order to underline the affirmation that it was possible to do so. Reading and writing can be very helpful here and sharing my own expressed thoughts in writing to benefit others, continues to help me to make progress.

3   **Learn to accept offers of help gracefully**

People really want to help in your loss and practical

help in the form of cooking and household chores in the early days should be accepted without guilt, for you are allowing others to feel that they are helping you. Even simple tasks like shopping are very difficult early on, especially as you are likely to bump into people you know in local stores.

Although there is the option to shop on-line these days, the concentration required for this is likely to be beyond you at first. I found I drove miles to avoid my local shops for fear of having to face people whom I knew and who would invariably ask me about James. My best help has always come from those who are prepared to listen if I wish to talk or sit quietly if I do not, who do not stand in judgement of where I am in my grief, those who empathise without trying to solve my problems (which of course they cannot). The best friend is one who sits with you regardless and accepts your febrile, inconsistent state without questioning it.

4   **Accept that other people do not understand**

You may be surprised by the insensitivity you encounter around you. It is necessary to learn ways not to let this upset you. People really do not mean it, but they cannot help trying to accommodate your loss by putting themselves in your shoes and offering reassurances, which always start with *"I know how you feel because …"* When clearly, they do not.

Worse than that are the times when people assume a stricken expression and say, *"Oh, you are so brave! I am sure I would just fall to pieces,"* or similar, implying that you have some magical strength.

This makes it very difficult to behave naturally with the other person and you find you need to assume a mask to conceal the feelings that you may have. Resilience and dogged determination seem to be more appropriate to me than actual bravery in terms of my loss.

I recall a conversation I was privy to not long after James died. One woman said, *"Oh, I can't wait for my kids to leave home, they are driving me mad. It wouldn't bother me if I never saw them again!"* I am afraid the nasty side of me wanted to say, *"Be careful what you wish for,"* but I managed not to. There is often an internal dialogue going on inside your head and it is probably just as well you do not say exactly what you are thinking, so as not to offend others!

There is a great deal of allowance-making for others that comes with the territory of grief – and it is tiring. I resented this greatly in the early days. It is not easy to offset this, but you come to realise that other people truly wish to help even if they cannot understand, and they do not intend to be insensitive.

5   **Embrace new friendships; they are gifts**

Early in your loss, your new friends are likely to be other bereaved people. These friendships are immensely special. They often endure and move beyond the initial awfulness which brought you together to become more 'normal' friendships where your shared bereavement is not the key factor in the friendship. But interestingly, I have found I have made other friendships, meeting people who are not bereaved parents but to whom I relate, and who have an understanding of loss because they themselves have experienced trauma of some kind.

It is always difficult to know when to introduce the topic of loss to a new relationship because it is necessarily difficult; it is impossible to know how people will react. There is a certain level of stigmatisation that comes with the territory of being bereaved.

As soon as you bring death into the conversation, there is a change in the dynamic of the situation. This is inevitable.

I have learned over the years that it is not always obligatory to reveal my loss to others. At first, it feels as though it must be visible, that I have been marked in some way by my experience, but these days I realise this is not the case.

Holidays, for example, can be a time of freedom to meet people and have discussions about children and family without revealing personal loss. I used to feel tremendously guilty about doing this but now I know it as a protective mechanism that is good for my emotional health. Importantly, I don't need to tell everyone I meet that my son died.

That is not to say I am denying his existence in any way; rather I am selective about the people with whom I share my experience.

My realisation over recent years has been quite an eye opener – which is that everyone has a story, and it may be not as bad, or it may be worse than mine, but we all have life events, stresses, traumas through which we can relate and help each other. I have met a great many people since losing James; paths have been crossed and events have happened which would not otherwise have occurred. I see all these new aspects to my life as gifts and welcome them as they happen; rather than constantly reverting to the reason why they happen.

6   **Don't dismiss counselling**

You may feel that counselling is not for you, and as a lay person it is difficult for me to judge how necessary it is in the grieving process. But being able to talk in a safe, supportive environment and express sentiments you may not be able to share with your nearest and dearest, to a listener who is trained to listen, can be very helpful. I can only speak from my own experience which was very positive. Informal counselling in the form of conversations with others going through loss is also immensely valuable. Anything that normalises your grieving process can only be good and healthy. My favourite form of informal counselling is to go for a long walk with a friend and talk out the emotions that need to be shared.

Attending relevant workshops, participating in helpful therapies such as meditation, joining groups both secular and spiritual that help you process loss: all these represent different types of counselling which are an option if you do not like the idea of formal therapy.

7   **Populate your own toolbox with positive elements**

Amassing helpful items in your toolbox is a pleasurable task.

You can choose whatever helps in your own particular circumstances and have a variety of different tools for varying situations. Your memories and the triggers for them are the most valuable things to treasure.

Your immediate reaction to loss may be to get rid of reminders, clear rooms and wardrobes as soon as possible. But be careful! – once they are gone, you cannot recover these items. It is very difficult to face tangible reminders at first, and my advice would be to put them out of sight for the time being until they can be approached.

My toolbox began and indeed continues to have as its main feature, my love of words and writing. *Into the Mourning Light* shared James's story with many people and when I am told that it brings comfort, I feel that is honouring James's memory too. James was a great one for helping people, and he would be thrilled to know that he is giving comfort to those who need it. The knowledge that my words help others, uplifts me in turn and I am grateful for the gift of written expression.

Even if you are not a writer, keeping a journal is very helpful. In particular, the new griever's memory is notoriously poor and looking back on a journal or diary is very helpful to demonstrate progress. I also populate my toolbox with the various projects in which I get involved, and it contains my leisure time pleasures – exercise, spiritual nourishment, photography and so on.

I am gratified to be able to be involved in workshops, sharing grief resources and helping raise water safety awareness with bereavement organisations and the RNLI, with a remit that reflects my desire to share the positive aspects of grief work.

I never imagined that I would become associated with a high-profile organisation such as the RNLI through the loss of James. It was soon after the publication of *Into the Mourning Light* that my connection began, through initial contact from Teddington helmsman Andy Butterfield, who read locally about my book.

In turn, Andy connected me with RNLI staff Guy Addington and Ross Macleod. I told James's story for the Respect the Water campaign in 2014 and was heavily involved in the campaign that year, as described later.

8   **Appreciate the world around you and look to the light**
The isolating nature of early grief means that you are so focused on yourself and your emotions that you miss what is happening around you. Although it is difficult when you are struggling to get through each day, it is important to plan future events to have something to look forward to. This brings huge guilt to begin with. You may ask yourself, "*What right do I have to feel happy/enjoy myself?*" but in fact it is far healthier

and better to push yourself outside your comfort zone and learn to enjoy life again.

I have always found the cycle of the seasons comforting and to go out for a walk and literally 'take time to smell the roses' is very nourishing to the soul. Planning time away gives a sense of moving forward. Going away brings a measure of relief from the day to day grind of grieving. It can, however, be difficult to come home and it takes time to restore a normal response in this regard. I used to dread coming home because walking through the front door and into an empty house underlined the absence of James. But now I hold close my memories of him and imagine how pleased he would be that his stepdad and I are travelling and enjoying new experiences in different parts of the world.

It has taken time to re-integrate ourselves into a social life with a degree of confidence. Equally, it has taken time for family and friends to appreciate that we are at ease with celebrations.

It is difficult to see your son's peers moving forward into adulthood, settling down, marrying, having children – but how much worse it would feel to be excluded from their joys and triumphs for fear that you will be upset.

People tend to tiptoe around the bereaved socially and this is something which I feel strongly should change if the taboo were to be taken out of the subject – when it is appropriate.

9   **Accept that the process of consolidating grief is entirely individual**

No single person can compare their grief journey to another's. There are some common denominators, of course, but the sense of grief and loss you feel cannot be defined and comprehended except by yourself.

The journey is long, hard and tortuous. But ultimately there is an element of satisfaction in realising that you may well in fact have experienced personal growth, strength and confidence arising from the travails of your loss.

Personally, I believe that all that I learned about grief and loss over the first ten years, has made me a better-rounded and more compassionate person, though I would never have chosen to embark on this particular learning curve.

10   **Appreciate that full acceptance may never come**

As a parent, I invariably ask the question: how is it possible to fully accept the loss of a child? However well you follow the tenets of the grieving process, do you really ever accept the loss? You may (eventually) be able to accept the loss of your own parents, a spouse, partner, sibling or peer, but there is no avoiding the fact that your children are not meant to die before you.

I prefer to use the words *assimilation* and *integration* to reflect my level of acceptance of my loss.

By integrating my loss, I can live meaningfully again.

I can fulfil my valued roles as a wife, mother, stepmother and grandparent with joy tempered with poignancy that does not overwhelm or detract from our future happiness.

I can take up the baton that James should have carried, in the time I have left, and carry it for him.

I feel thankful for the nineteen years that I was blessed to know my son.

I hope those close to me see that my loss lives alongside me in its rightful place rather than the loss defining who I am.

I feel a huge regret for all the years of life that are denied to James, but I no longer mourn his loss in the way I did at the beginning. That level of traumatic distress becomes ultimately futile and damaging to the future not just for myself, but for those around me.

My remit remains to deal with my grief as positively and usefully as possible. I had no idea I would learn so much from it, nor be able to share it in helpful ways, and for these gifts in loss I am grateful.

When you are daily focusing so intently on your feelings, you need to take a break from all the intensity surrounding your grief. After all, you can't be permanently analysing how you feel, where you are on your personal emotional barometer and so on.

This is where a bit of altruism can come in. This is where you release some of the introspection and begin to look outwards. You have already garnered hope and light about yourself. Now you can begin to utilise these in ways you never imagined. Marcel Proust said:[3] *"We don't receive wisdom; we must discover it for ourselves after a journey that no one can take for us, or spare us."* These are true words. The learning curve following bereavement is steep and painful, but you definitely do learn and acquire confidence and skills you never imagined would be at your fingertips.

I am often struck anew by the sheer number of people who have engaged with me in one way or another since the beginning. It is true to say that social media has played a great part in my being able to communicate with many more people than would ordinarily be possible, too. When James died, the internet was one of the first places where I sought to learn more about this alien planet called bereavement. I continue to use it on a daily basis. When I publish a blog post or post onto Facebook and Twitter, the internet allows for contact with people all around the world in an instant.

Communication through all forms of media, constantly reinforcing messages and taking the taboo out of issues surrounding death, grief and loss is ultimately a helpful and supportive tool for anyone who is grieving.

I see that my role in water safety has gradually become twofold. Firstly, I understand the importance of telling James's story – not to sensationalise, but to personalise, the reality of living the life of a bereaved parent, also how that impacts on the family and beyond. My work with Kingston Council, my writing and my subsequent involvement with the RNLI and other organisations are all key to sharing very important messages around the matters of water safety.

Secondly, I feel it is vital to share and talk about the issues surrounding trauma, grief and loss, for our own health and wellbeing. It is well recognised that acquiring a grief toolbox is key to getting through the worst of times and remaining relatively sane!

I welcome the chance to share these aspects of grieving whenever possible, through writing, presentations and workshops.

Chapter 4

New Connections

The stages of grief are non-linear, it seems to me. After a while, even when they continue to appear, there arrives a new kind of confidence in the life of the griever. This is subtle, but it underpins the twists and turns of life's ongoing pattern. A sense that we have hit the nadir and are creeping slowly back, and that though we will have further trials to face, there is a level of bedrock that we will know is there, even in the darkest moments. Andrea Corrie

After the publicity surrounding the release of *Into the Mourning Light* in 2014, I was particularly touched to hear from two friends of James who were on his course at Brighton Uni in 2004. The first wrote to say that James most definitely isn't forgotten, and he is remembered with 'such fondness.' I think it is fair to say that all bereaved parents have the recurring nightmare that their child will be forgotten, and to be told this is not the case by someone who only knew James for the year he was at University is immensely helpful.

Kim, who is now a PE teacher in Cambridgeshire wrote:

"Hi Andrea. I just read about your book and shed a tear as memories came flooding back. James was at Brighton University studying the same course as me. Our paths would have crossed more as the degree continued and I am

sad I did not get to spend more time with him. When I turned the page of the newspaper and saw his photo on Brighton seafront, the memories of that era came back.

The children in my class will always know about water safety and be reminded of how precious life is.

I cannot imagine your loss. James was a credit to you and your family and I agree he would have made a wonderful teacher. Sorry to have rambled on to you but reading your article has given me an outlet and some perspective."

This wonderful message carries its own amazing legacy from James. Now and in the future, more young people will be aware of the dangers of water, thanks to Kim's compassion and the fact that she knew James. It is so very heartening.

Kim's commitment to water safety was further underlined when she recently wrote about the present situation in her workplace, a school in the Cambridgeshire Fens:

"As I entered the classroom to a sea of eagerly awaiting faces, I dared to believe that this year may be different from the previous few. As the Year 6 Standard Assessment Tests loom, I always like to be prepared for those exciting few months which follow. Impromptu rounders matches, a class play and lots of treats after all the hard work. This year I also have a new plan.

"So, who in here considers themselves a non-swimmer?"

I'm met with blank faces, no hands in the air. This is great, maybe last year was a blip. As I start to explain further, "This means no feet touching the bottom, no holding on to the side" …more hands start to go up. Too many hands, in fact.

Since taking on my new role as head of PE in a primary school, it has become frighteningly clear that swimming and water safety has taken a back seat. Schools, especially in the remote villages around where I live, are struggling to get children to the local pool for a good quality lesson. The children swim for six weeks of the year in Years 3-6. It's better than nothing but without extra lessons or water experience outside of school, it just isn't enough.

Take for example our recent class of Year 4's. In a class of 36 children, 24 were non-swimmers and they shared a swimming instructor in the shallow end. Of these 24, six were hanging off the poor teaching assistant, too terrified to let go. This breaks my heart but at the same time makes me quite angry.

Maybe I was lucky. My primary school had its own swimming pool. We swam from reception class to Year 6 and by the time I was eleven I could self-rescue wearing pyjamas and had completed my two-mile distance award. My parents took me swimming when they could and on family holidays, we always spent time by water. Don't get me wrong; I expected there to be a few children who couldn't swim when I asked, those who hadn't had the experience of family holidays, swimming lessons etc. But this feels different.

My own son is three years old and he swims weekly with me. He has had no formal lessons but has been taken to a range of swimming pools since he was two months old. He is confident in the water and is so excited about getting in that he more often than not gets himself changed into his swimwear and opens the changing room door before I can get my shoes off! Watching him in the water makes me extremely proud but also seeing the sheer joy on his face is something every parent should strive to achieve. I never want to see him scared, nor for him to miss out on pool parties, holiday water parks and trips. I am confident my son will look forward to swimming lessons at school; however, when I see almost half a class dreading this part of the week and feigning illness just to stay away from the water, it's clear that things need to change.

I teach in a supportive school in the heart of the Cambridgeshire fens. We are surrounded by water with lakes, ditches, cut off channels: all just on my short journey to work. It terrifies me to think that should a stray football land in the park pond, or a child fall out of a dinghy playing in the sea, that it could end in utter heartbreak, unless more is done.

I have put aside money from my PE budget to try anything to help our children to be safe around water. With National guidelines recommending that children leave primary school able to swim competently, confidently and proficiently over a distance of at least 25 metres and perform safe self-rescue in different water-based situations, unless parents make that extra effort to get their children used to water, it will not happen.

I think of James often when I'm supporting swimming lessons at school, or when I'm watching my son play in shallows. This year thirteen children will leave my school unable to swim. Sixteen were offered free 'booster' swimming lessons I had arranged for them to achieve this very important life skill. Sadly, and quite depressingly, only six were sent to school with a swimming kit and a permission letter."

I was also contacted on Facebook by Gemma, one of James's college friends.

80

She made some lovely comments, including,

"As so many others have said to you, James really did touch my life. I have some photos of him from those sixth form years ...James always looked handsome and had a big grin on his face! ... I treasure these ... before the advent of the camera phone I am glad that I had at some point had an actual camera and taken actual films to the actual shop!"

Best of all, Gemma sent me a number of images which I was happy to share online.

What a gift! – seeing those happy, joyous moments of James's life when he was simply sharing fun with a friend. Yes, it makes me sad to know that they were finite moments, but it is still a pleasure to see them and vicariously share in his happiness from the time they were taken.

Gemma also said, *"James would have loved the selfie craze."* And I concur entirely with that. He would have been one of the first people to buy a selfie stick, definitely!

And I bless the fact that Gemma, like other friends of James, kept the photos because they still mean something to them, he was a part of their story too.

When I was making the final edits to this chapter, I invited Gemma to share a little of how her feelings have changed with the passage of time and she very kindly wrote for me:

"James's friendship has definitely stayed with me through the years. However, with an increasingly hectic schedule and the infinite distractions life brings, I'm guilty in saying that although I may not think of him every day anymore,

it is most certainly often. Occasionally he'll appear in a dream, which I adore; I wish I was a firmer believer in the spiritual world, but I confidently attribute these visits to his firm position in my subconscious brain and long-term memories - my heart and my soul. And I take equal comfort from that as if I could believe it were something more divine.

Places, songs, people, situations, TV shows; all sorts of things bring him to mind and it is always with a warm feeling and no longer with that sickening sense of sorrow. I hope he would be glad about that; with the passage of time it is not a forgetting about the person but an evolving process of reflection.

This has undoubtedly been helped along by natural aging and maturing, becoming a mother myself and processing new losses and experiences.

However, the regular little snippets of memory which are brought about, mostly out of the blue, take me right back to that time, being the carefree teens we were, and that brings joy now, not sadness. I think that is the greatest change that the passing of time has brought about: the sadness I experience now is less that of raw loss but that of what James would have become, what he would be doing now, where he would be in his career, would he have children? He would certainly adore his nieces and nephews. Where would he live? What role would he have in my life? What advice would he give me? These musings are endless, as are the places, voices, smells and sounds that evoke them. I can say they bring a bittersweet comfort now, because remembering him and his life, and our times together, only brings joy."

These friends of James may have been anxious that they might upset me. But it is true to say that any new reminders of James do not make me sad; rather they are like gifts dropped into my loss.

The contacts are like little nudges from James, virtual visits that bring warmth to my heart.

In all my dealings with the RNLI, from the campaign work to support during my talks at the College in Poole and during the making of a video film, everyone involved has been incredibly helpful and kind.

I take the view that the work of the RNLI itself is made up of acts of kindness.

After all, what could be a kinder act than to voluntarily put your life on the line to save someone else's?

The ethos of all who volunteer for and work with the RNLI is a sincere desire to improve water safety universally and to prevent unnecessary loss of life. The men and women of the RNLI leave ego outside the door and concentrate on the tasks they face in an utterly commendable way, often in challenging and perilous circumstances.

I don't have the training or expertise of the RNLI lifeguards; I am just one individual striving to make a difference where I can. Should I ever doubt the validity of what I am doing in this regard, the following incident reinforces that I am indeed helping.

When our Australian friend Karen was staying with us in 2014, we went to Kingston riverside so she could see for herself the place I had described to her in writing and images.

It was something of an emotional pilgrimage, of course, but there was also comfort in sharing and it was lovely to be able to show Karen the physical reality of Kingston, rather than images. We walked and talked together and were rewarded by an unusual sight – the Royal Barge passed along the river just as we reached the point of really needing a lift to our spirits.

We stood by the barriers and I gazed out across the river, thinking of James and just being in the moment.

Karen nudged me. *"Look,"* she said, *"Watch that family."*

I became aware of a man, woman and two young boys who had walked past us. The man stopped to look at the RNLI Respect the Water 'Tonne of Water' installation. (This is a water filled model which illustrates the weight and size of a ton of water and was being used as a message in the campaign). The man called back his family.

Karen and I were not close enough to hear their entire conversation, but it was easy to guess it from their expressions and their body language, *"Look at this, boys, you should read it and take note..."*

The boys duly read the words, each tried ineffectually to push the installation, pitting their boyish shoulders against it and grinning ruefully when they couldn't move it.

Meanwhile, Karen and I guessed that the woman we

assumed was the boys' mum was reading James's memorial plaque; she looked pensively out across the water for a moment.

The family spent several minutes examining the installation, reading the text, and evidently giving it some serious consideration before they moved onward.

Briefly, I was tempted to approach them and tell them of its significance... but it felt wrong to do so and it would have brought down the entire family's day.

On this occasion it was sufficient to have such strong visual evidence that our work at Kingston is not over and done with. It continues, thanks to the RNLI and the other authorities who are involved in making our riverside a safer place for future generations.

Sometimes, significant moments arrive in your life when you least expect them. You may not even recognise them for what they are; small in themselves, these are acts of generosity of spirit that resonate deep within and leave a long-lasting impression.

One such pivotal moment - during a surreal day in May 2015 - was not, as you might imagine, when I walked across the stage at London's Barbican to receive the RNLI Individual Supporter award, presented by HRH the Duke of Kent.

Nor was it when the immensely professional and moving

videos made by the RNLI, including the film of our story, were screened prior to the presentations.

It was not even when, earlier in the day, a fellow awardee and I were interviewed on ITV's *Lorraine* programme, though that was about as far away from my norm as I could get.

No …the moment came as, rather shakily, I returned to my seat in the Barbican Theatre, clutching the award, heart pounding and throat tight with emotion. (For ease of access to the stage, the award recipients were seated separately so my husband Shaun was sitting in a different part of the auditorium).

I became aware of someone looking at me … a woman I didn't know, seated a couple of rows away. Our eyes met and I guessed she could see I was just about holding it together. She quickly moved across into the seat next to me and grasped my hand in both of hers.

"You shouldn't be on your own right now," she whispered against the backdrop of commentary from the stage,

"Are you OK, is there anyone I can get for you?"

"I am all right," I replied. *"My husband is just over there. I'm fine, really!"*

I don't think she was convinced, she sat next to me simply comforting me by her presence and continuing to hold tightly onto my hand.

"I lost my brother a long time ago, when he was just fourteen," she went on, *"So I know a little of the emotion you must be feeling."*

We sat together for a little longer before this big-hearted RNLI volunteer, satisfied that I was going to be all right on my own, moved back to her seat.

The whole episode was over in a matter of minutes, but it exemplifies the immense generosity of spirit and kind-heartedness that I have encountered, almost across the board, in the years since James died. Naturally, people want to empathise; but they cannot possibly understand traumatic loss unless they have walked a similar road, however well-intentioned they are.

Initially, I was embarrassed by the thought of the RNLI award. I am not a centre stage player as a rule.

It was pointed out to me that this recognition reflects not only my contribution to the Respect the Water campaign, but also the impact of our three years of commitment to Kingston Council, that resulted in significant river safety improvements and a reduction in the number of water-related incidents in the area.

James's legacy had begun.

Following on from my work with the Respect the Water campaign, I was invited to share what happened to James as a written Case Study within the National Water Safety Forum strategy document. This was being prepared by the

RNLI and other contributory organisations. I agreed, and over the months I received updates on how the initiative was progressing through the consultation process.

One day, an email popped into my inbox. To my great surprise, it contained a rather special invitation, and that is how Shaun and I found ourselves in esteemed company at the House of Commons one February evening in 2016.

We arrived in the wonderful historic surroundings of Parliament and at 7pm around 60 people gathered together on the Pavilion Terrace, overlooking the Thames.

It was good to re-establish contact with some of the RNLI staff whom I have met before as well as meeting representatives from organisations including the Maritime and Coastguard Agency, Amateur Swimming Association, Chief Fire Officers' Association, Royal Life Saving Society and RoSPA.

The formal part of the launch reception consisted of three speeches:

George Rawlinson, Operations Director of the RNLI and Chair of the Forum, shared the shocking statistic that up to 400 people drown in the UK each year and a further 200 take their own lives on our waters. He emphasised that a collaborative approach is essential if the National Water Safety Forum is to achieve its objective of a future without drowning.

The key aim is to halve the number of drownings by 2026 through better prevention, education, targeting specific groups and reducing risks to the community.

The launch of the strategy was undoubtedly a strong call to action – a call to make contributing to national goals a local priority.

Dr David Meddings, representing the World Health Organisation, adopts a humanitarian approach to the problem and his vision is to see an NWSF plan being adopted in every country, aiming to reduce the global problem.

Finally, Minister Robert Goodwill, then the Minister for Transport and MP for Scarborough and Whitby, told the audience that through his ministerial role, he had been able to award almost £1 million of government funds to 51 UK charities to support water rescue services in local communities.

This additional exposure through my connection with the organisation, underlined how blessed I feel to have come within the radar of the RNLI, and to be given repeated opportunities to share the positive and far-reaching outcomes that have resulted from the dreadful catalyst of losing James. The impact of the constructive changes that have been made at Kingston riverside continues to echo ever wider which is something I did not anticipate at the time we completed our campaign.

At the House of Commons event I met Dawn Whittaker, now Chief Fire Officer and Chief Executive for East Sussex Fire & Rescue Service (ESFRS).

In her own words, Dawn says that she *"pledges to continue to do all I can through my Chief Fire Officers' Association role and within my power locally to support and influence change, improve communication and achieve a reduction in drownings and to work with all agencies to raise awareness."*

The ESFRS has the same aims and intention as the National Water Safety Forum: to halve the number of drownings which occur in waters in and around the UK, by 2026.

It is easy to see the relevance of the involvement of the Fire and Rescue service alongside those organisations more easily identifiable as being involved with water safety, such as the RNLI, the Royal Life Saving Society and HM Coastguard.

My view, strengthened over the time since James died, is that drowning prevention must begin with education, and a heightened awareness by every young person that they have to look out for their own and their peers' safety, with diligence.

Every child will ultimately have the opportunity to learn to swim. It is important (if obvious) to note that being able to swim does not preclude drowning, as we know to our cost.

But it is not just about children being able to swim. I was asked recently *"What do you think, from a personal perspective, can really make a significant difference?"* And my response is this:

"It is not enough simply to teach children to swim. They need to have an awareness of the dangers associated with the most benign looking water. They need to carry that awareness with them wherever they go, so that they have the same respect for their own safety whether they are in a local swimming pool or on a beach overseas. My hope is that constant reinforcement of water safety messages could ultimately lead to a trigger to the mind – something that would sound an alarm in the brain when approaching a dangerous situation, to stop it going any further."

I also feel, very strongly, a growing sense that up until recently, organisations have been lax in recognising the needs of their own staff who are working 'at the sharp end' and dealing with very traumatic circumstances. To this end, I always advocate that people seek their own avenues of grief and trauma support after incidents.

These days it is easy to access bereavement support organisations such as The Compassionate Friends, CRUSE, the Drowning Support Network and SOBS (Survivors of Bereavement by Suicide) to name but a few, and there is a definite need to make these easily accessible to operational staff as well as families at the appropriate time through the available links.

Subsequent to another talk at the launch of the RNLI Fish Supper charity fundraiser in October 2016 (described in Chapter 10) I paid a return visit to the College in Poole in January 2017, this time to speak at a training event.

My brief was to address a new group of operational RNLI Managers with specific responsibilities covering the entire coast, including Irish waters and the River Thames. This is a group of men and women who together have an enormous amount of knowledge and experience within their specific fields.

Prior to the presentation, which was to start at 5pm, Shaun and I were sitting with a cup of tea in the Slipway café bar at the RNLI College, watching through the window a group of starlings, known as a murmuration.

We marvelled at their airborne acrobatics as they gracefully swirled, swooped and dipped, forming wonderful shapes which morphed and changed with smooth fluidity in the sky above the water in the bay.

Their synchrony and grace were a delight, and we felt privileged to be watching their spectacular pre-roost show, as the light was fading fast.

One theory of such murmurations is that they are to do with defence, representing distraction and safety in numbers; the group behaving with a single purpose, and in the starlings' case, to avoid predators.

But perhaps one of the most interesting aspects of the birds' behaviour in formation is that the group responds as one.

Although they are separate, entirely individual characters, they move collectively, forming their shapes in shared commonality.

As I come to know better the men and women associated with the RNLI, whether they are volunteers or staff, it is not too fanciful to think that collectively they behave much like a murmuration.

Apart from the fact that they are not in danger from marauding raiders – although of course they experience negativity from a few detractors – their underlying aim and remit is single-mindedly purposeful and can be summed up in their inherent desire to make our waters safe for everyone. They are entirely impartial, proactive, positive personalities whose aims and aspirations I cannot praise highly enough. They are vocational and often generational, many of them having fathers and grandfathers who served the RNLI. The water is in their blood and it shows in their passionate commitment to make a difference.

What could I, as an individual, tell them that would impact on the group?

I felt the most value I could bring to the presentation would be to share my own reality of What Happens Next;

by which I mean … how do you live your life after the crushing loss of a beloved son to accidental drowning? It is only through my dealings with the RNLI that I have come to understand how important it is to keep telling our personal story. This is because the ways in which sharing some of James, and our life as it has evolved since his loss, provide insight into the stark reality of being a bereaved parent.

The things we do as we go through our lives can outlast our own mortality. The things we do today and tomorrow are stepping stones, always building for the future.

Sharing our memories and our present and our potential future provides unexpected legacies for those whom we have lost. I am indebted to the RNLI for allowing me to continue telling the story. There is naturalness in the murmurations of the starlings.

There is naturalness in the ebb and flow of our seas and waterways which commands us to remain vigilant and always to continue to Respect the Water.

I have also had opportunities to address other groups about bereavement.

Following a presentation in 2010 I was invited by CRUSE to address a group of around 20 volunteers in training in November 2014.

My remit was to speak about what is truly like to live

with the loss of a child. I prepared a presentation that summarised James's story and how we manage the years of loss. I spoke honestly and described the holistic approach that I adopt in trying to live with grief as best I can.

The CRUSE presentation was well received, and we had an active and honest question and answer session afterwards. I had been asked also to prepare some do's and don'ts for counsellors and others to use when they encounter bereaved families:

- Don't tell them that such tragedies happen to only those who are strong enough to survive them
- Don't change the subject when they mention their child
- Don't stop mentioning their child's name because you are scared of reminding them: you cannot upset them any more than they have already been upset
- Don't presume to understand their grief because you have experienced the death of an elderly relative or even a pet
- Don't remind them that they have other children or could have another child
- Don't say *"I don't know how you cope; I couldn't."* The bereaved have no choice in the matter.
- Do be as normal as possible with them; talking about ordinary things and even sitting in silence, can be

comforting

- Do allow them to talk about the person who died, which sounds an obvious point, but too often we sidestep mentioning anything associated with death and dying.

- Talking about the person who has passed can really help the griever to utilise this emotional safety valve.

- Do answer questions honestly and understand that while some people have a need to know small details, others will only want the wider picture

- Do ask how they are feeling, but only if you are prepared to listen to the answer

- Do express your own sadness about what has happened, and encourage them to talk about him or her as often as they want

- Do remember the needs of surviving brothers and sisters and the wider family who may all need support and ask you questions that they cannot ask the parents

- Do remember that you must protect yourself from being drained by the needs of the bereaved family – who heals the healer?

A surprising offshoot of that CRUSE presentation came some little while afterwards. During my presentation I spoke of how helpful and cathartic it is to write out one's feelings. Most people, even if they think they cannot write, find that they can express themselves in the written word if they set up a scenario that works for them. For example, I like to write with music in the background. Others prefer silence or to sit in a café and have ambient noise around. I suggested the counsellors think about writing as a self-help tool when they are considering how they are managing themselves emotionally, in dealing with their clients' problems. I pointed out that one of the kindest things you can do for someone who is grieving is to send them a simple note. In our digital age, a few words on a card mean even more. Writing can be as personal and private as you wish. Many people keep journals that are never intended to be shared or write letters to people that are never sent. The mere act of writing can be cathartic and therapeutic whether or not it is disseminated.

A while after the CRUSE talk, one of the attendees, Christine, sent me an email telling me that following my presentation, she had written her first ever poem for a friend after she lost her son to a car accident. This she kindly shared with me and with her permission I reproduce it here. It is a touching and emotive tribute to her friend's son and underlines what I am fond of saying, *"Never say you can't do something. Never say never!"*

'Poem written for a friend

Your loss is so hard to bear
Now that L is no longer there
The deep black void that fills your days
Seems never ending
But remember all the joy he brought
When the darkness is too hard to bear
Remember all the fun you had
It will always be there
Look up when you can and see his light
Shining on you strong and bright
He is now safe and beyond pain
Where are you now? - not the same
Grief has changed you beyond measure
Let his memory be your treasure
How can you take his light into the world?
What in you waits to be unfurled?
When you meet again and he asks what did you do
What will you tell him? — that you died with him that terrible day
Or that you lived on in a different way
What that is you may not know yet
But when the dark void becomes too great
Think how you can use it — to create - another different way of being
All compassionate and all seeing.'

Receiving feedback like this after a talk validates many of
the reasons why I feel it is so important to share the many
features of grieving and how they can be channelled into
a positive outcome.

I am at times called 'brave' and 'strong' for all the work that I have done since James left us.

If strength is the inherent capacity to manifest energy, to endure and to resist, then my strength has grown over the years.

If bravery reflects courage and valour, then I possess a measure of this.

But whilst I am grateful for the accolades, I believe that I am lucky to have the resilience that allows me to channel my energies into the achievement of significant outcomes.

I could not possibly have done any of this without the support of Shaun, my family and my friends, who provide unstinting backing and encouragement in all that I do.

My water safety advocacy work continues. In 2017, another honour was bestowed on James's memory via the dedication of a throw bag training manual in his name. This was a first for the RNLI and made me incredibly proud.

In March 2019 I was invited to speak about the impact of loss at a collaborative meeting arranged by the Surrey Fire and Rescue Service and RNLI – another step forward in education and drowning prevention under the umbrella of the National Water Safety Forum. In turn this led to my doing some publicity work with the London Fire Brigade who are extending their remit to incorporate water safety issues.

Following this, I was among the invited guests boarding the Silver Sturgeon, a splendid river cruiser, at HMS President in London on Tuesday 21 May 2019. The event was the launch of the Tidal Thames Water Safety Forum's Drowning Prevention Strategy. In a unique collaboration, The Port of London Authority, The Metropolitan Police, London Fire Brigade, Royal National Lifeboat Institution, London Ambulance Service and Maritime & Coastguard Agency have come together to produce a Drowning Prevention Strategy for the tidal Thames along its 95-mile course, from Teddington to the North Sea.

It is a sad fact that although the number of accidental water incidents is gradually reducing, there is a rise in the number of people intentionally entering the water for purposes of harm.

Each organisation pledges its individual contribution to the strategy which has evolved in part from the National Drowning Prevention Strategy.

The **scope** of the Forum is to prevent accidental and self-harm drownings in the Thames by working in partnership.

The **aim** of the Forum is to reduce the number of deaths in and on the tidal Thames by targeting a strategy of 'zero harm.'

In the run up to the day, there was a high level of

confidentiality surrounding the identity of the principal guest, HRH Prince William, the Duke of Cambridge, and I had been sworn to secrecy! It was difficult not to feel excited at the prospect of meeting a member of the Royal family who would have a significant influence on the impact of the strategy.

I had been invited to the event along with Beckie Ramsay, who is also a bereaved mother and water safety advocate. Beckie is an ardent campaigner in memory of her son Dylan, whose life was taken in an accident in a gravel pit local to their home in Lancashire in 2011. With the tragic link of our similar loss in common, we made contact via social media and arranged to meet in London. We spent the evening before the meeting talking about James and Dylan, preparing ourselves as best we could for the prospect of the following day.

HRH The Duke of Cambridge had specifically asked to speak with families who knew the impact of losing a loved one to drowning, and Beckie and I were to have the privilege of a personal conversation with him at the end of the meeting, after the formal presentations.

We were blessed with clear blue skies and London sparkled in the sunshine on the day. A short taxi ride brought us to HMS President and from there, all the guests boarded the Silver Sturgeon.

Beckie and I waited nervously in the boat's salon for the Duke's arrival. He was brought on board and introduced to representatives of the partner organisations before coming to meet us. A member of the Royal household gave us a few tips on protocol and suddenly, he was approaching us – it was rather a surreal moment!

The Duke sat down at a table with us and after our introductions, his opening comment was,

"Gosh, what a lovely warm morning, I had to take off my jumper!"

Such an ordinary opener to conversation put us at our ease and Beckie and I were able to talk to him about Dylan and James. We were able to emphasise the importance of water safety awareness and drowning prevention from our individual and personal perspectives.

As the conversation between the three of us was private, it would be wrong to reprise it, but I will say that throughout the time we had, it was obvious that the Duke was listening intently and Beckie and I could see that he had great empathy for our situations. His comments were insightful, and he was easy to talk to.

The Samaritans were represented at the launch. Jonny Benjamin, whose suicide was effectively prevented by passer by Neil Laybourn in 2008, gave moving testimony to the power of simple conversation to save a life. This was further emphasised by the Duke of Cambridge who said, *"A simple 'Hello, how are you?' is sometimes all it takes to save a life."*

Much networking ensued during the boat trip that followed, and I enjoyed new introductions and re-acquaintance with members of the partner organisations.

I am sure I also speak for Beckie when I express how much we appreciated the warmth, kindness and support shown to us by everyone with whom we came into contact throughout the day.

Sharing a traumatic tragic event is never easy. It does not matter how much time has passed; the initial telling of the story is invariably a tug on the heart. But the ability to introduce our sons' names into so many other people's lives can only bring positive results.

Raising awareness of the danger of any body of water, however innocuous it looks, remains key to the objectives of any present and future strategy.

Every life lost to water is a life too many.

Every life lost to water affects an immeasurable number of people.

Parents like Beckie and I - indeed, any parents who have lost dearly loved children are best placed to understand the truly awful impact of our loss. By sharing our stories and raising the profile of the surrounding issues, we draw something positive out of our tragedy. Our heartfelt desire to prevent others experiencing the heartache that we live with on a daily basis is validated to an extent by strong calls to action such as this strategy. We cannot change the past, but we can influence the future.

When I come within the realm of such committed individuals as those whom I have met and connected with in these years, it is not difficult to accede to appeals for help through my emphasis of the personal impact of loss. I believe this is a valuable tool for prevention of future drowning tragedies. After my most recent talk in October 2019, one of the delegates asked me, *"how long do you think you will continue giving such presentations; do you anticipate a time when you will reach a point of drawing a line in the sand, and stop?"* It is an interesting question.

I must admit, I have never thought of a timeline. Although we are in the fifteenth year since losing James, my memories of July 2005 remain as clear and sharp as ever. Every bereaved parent will recognise this clarity of memory. It is only by having some distance from that time, that I am able to talk about it usefully and calmly; minus the rollercoaster effect of early grief plunging me into the darkest of places.

In effect, I don't see a cut-off point to my talks but I hope I will recognise it to be appropriate if and when that time comes. As long as I am able to help others learn about the smoothest path possible through loss, then I am glad to share my thoughts and experiences.

Everything that I do in honour of James's memory helps me to cope with the idea of his not being here anymore. Despite time passing, it still feels improbable that we will never see him again, that his footfall will not be heard on the path nor his key in the front door. Sadly, however many new connections are made, that can never change.

Chapter 5
Found by Faith

"When you have reached your own room, be kind to those who have chosen different doors and to those who are still in the hall. If they are wrong, they need your prayers all the more; and if they are your enemies, then you are under orders to pray for them. That is one of the rules common to the whole house." C S Lewis

For those who are not interested in discussion of religious conviction, this chapter may be viewed as optional reading. However, if you choose to read on, you will gain a better understanding of the intertwining of many strands, contributing to how my life has been shaped, particularly since losing James.

I will never be that religious anathema - a Bible-thumping, avidly churchgoing, God-bothering, evangelical Christian, set to convert everyone I know. My faith is quiet and filled with gratitude. I share it without imposition of any of my beliefs or ideology on anybody else. I have discovered just a few of the many ways in which belonging to a religion can help with the bleak aftermath of loss. I believe there is much in faith to help us find the light that lies beyond our darkest moments.

It is true to say that in part, I have modern technology to

thank for setting me off into faith exploration. The first signposting along the way came about when I began to listen to the Radio 2 programme, *Good Morning Sunday*, some few years ago, on 'catch up.' Tired of the forced jollity and the advertising of early morning commercial radio, instead I listened to GMS each week over the course of four or five days and heard a small segment of the programme in the morning when I was getting ready to go to work. I soon realised that I enjoyed hearing the views of the faith guests on the show, who range from the Queen's Chaplain, Canon Ann Easter, through Rabbi Pete Tobias to Buddhists, Sikhs and others who represent many religions and faiths.

The periodic book reviews led me to new reading and I also enjoy the music which is a varied mix but often has a faith basis.

The guests who appear on the show all have interesting backgrounds and stories to tell and I learned a great deal about the attributes of personal resilience and faith of individuals in times of extremis.

I was incredibly moved by the true story of Judith Tebbut[1] who was held hostage in Somalia for six months after she and her husband were attacked by a group of armed pirates. David was murdered, but Judith did not know that he was dead until her son had the dreadful task of telling her in a brief telephone call when she had been in captivity for the first few, appalling weeks.

She retained throughout an extraordinary determination to survive and said that hope was her saviour.

People like Jude who do not bang on about their faith, but evidently have an unswerving belief that they will ultimately survive the greatest traumas that life can throw at them, have my greatest admiration. They are examples to those of us who do not find ourselves in such life-threatening extreme circumstances and they bring the realisation that our innate resilience, hope, and faith can make the most positive difference to our lives as we move forward.

But the pivotal person whom I first heard on GMS and who continues to be my main faith inspiration is Australian writer, speaker and broadcaster Sheridan Voysey. I heard him speak about his book *Resurrection Year²*, published in 2013, which he wrote after he and his wife tried for a full decade to have a baby. Disappointment and disillusionment heaped upon them, and even led to their questioning their hitherto strong faith. Eventually it became clear that the miracle they longed for was not going to happen. They took stock and decided to make a huge life move.

Sheridan's wife Merryn got a job as a medical statistician at Oxford University and Sheridan ultimately decided to write about what had happened to them.

"In retrospect," I heard Sheridan say, *"There is life after a dream has died. The God of the Crucifixion is also the God of the resurrection."*

As I listened to him for the first time, I was struck by the wonderful way he has with words. He is a man of soul and compassion.

He has empathy and understanding, he talks with the conviction of someone whose intrinsic faith underpins his thoughts and reasoning.

He has a lively, enquiring mind and a great sense of humour.

When he speaks of faith, he expresses himself in contemporary language and the more I hear and read his words, the greater is my admiration for him.

He is about as far away from my former idea of devout Christianity as it is possible to get.

Sheridan has my gratitude for opening my mind to new avenues.

His next book, published in 2015 resounded heartily with me, not least because of its title, *Resilient*[3], and I write more of this in Chapter 8. I became a bit of a Sheridan groupie! - following his podcasts and articles, finding myself increasingly drawn to his particular brand of down to earth and sensible Christianity.

I also met him briefly at a Christian worship event in

Somerset in 2018. It was a delight to have him sign my copy of *Resilient* and in return, to be able to sign a copy of *Into the Mourning Light* for him. I had never had such an opportunity before and it was, for this humble author, a very exciting thing to do!

Something about the way Sheridan describes his own faith underlines to me how a person's spirituality is not simply a blind leap, but is underpinned by evidence, and the unswerving belief that God is guiding us through all aspects of life.

Sheridan is a superb example of someone who lives a Christian life with no false modesty about admitting it. Although even he has to examine, question and explore his faith, which he does in his latest book. I knew that *The Making of Us*[4], published in March 2019, would be a different, more personal read to *Resilient*. What I was not prepared for was to read such an honest account of Sheridan's struggles with his faith, his identity and how he perceives his future legacy.

My personal view is to see Sheridan as a man of God, an instrument in sharing the word about Christianity without imposition on people who are not inclined to his views. His is usually a gentle take on faith, so it was quite a shock to read about his very deep self-examination and reflection while he and his friend DJ walked their difficult path of pilgrimage from Lindisfarne to Durham. Without revealing too much of the book's message, I was glad to ultimately be left with a sense of hope and optimism by the end of the journey. Sheridan's literal soul-baring is courageous and thought-provoking.

Now ... it's time for me to come out of the closet. The Alpha closet, that is.

Anglican priest Nicky Gumbel is the founder of the Alpha course, which since its inception in 1990 as a short course at his church, the Holy Trinity in London's Brompton Road, has gone global and relies on the basics of food, talks and conversation, all provided free of charge. Alpha is described as *a practical introduction to the Christian faith designed primarily for non-churchgoers and new Christians.* The only investment required is to turn up, and there is no pressure on you to confirm, or otherwise, whether or not you return week by week.

Alpha introduces those who wish to know more about the Christian faith to questions such as '*Who is Jesus? Why and how do I pray? How can I be filled with the Holy Spirit?*' The Alpha course is described as representing so-called charismatic church, being quite evangelical in nature.

I was first drawn to Alpha through curiosity, as I had no idea what it was. Driving to work, I daily passed a large United Reformed Church which had the Alpha Banner outside, with the question, '*Is there more to life than this? Find out with Alpha.*' I put 'Alpha' into a Google search and, given that I do love a course! - considered that it may well be something of interest to me.

Hence a cold January evening in 2016 found me in the nervous company of several others at Christchurch in Woking. We were made most welcome by the facilitators of the course, and soon discovered that ex Alpha students were happy to endorse the course and inspire us with their own take on what Alpha meant to them.

I loved the format of Alpha.

The sociability of the meal beforehand, the short DVD clip and structured talk and the final break off into smaller groups to have a conversation about the evening's theme were all equally palatable. Any fears that I had of the course being preachy, dogmatic, and overly zealous were quickly dispelled.

As the daughter of Jewish parents who were reasonably observant in my formative years, I had initially to get past a massive obstacle. For the first few Alpha evenings, I was haunted by an image of my father telling me, "*No dear, you mustn't believe in Jesus. He may have been a man who existed, perhaps a fisherman or a carpenter but he was definitely not the Son of God. And how could he die and live again? Hmph, impossible!*"

Half-remembered conversations with dad came back to

me as I recalled arguing semantics with him when I had been taught about the nativity at school. My brother went to lessons for his Bar Mitzvah and I occasionally went to the Jewish equivalent of Sunday school at the Synagogue, learning a little about the Old Testament and a small amount of Hebrew.

But it was a tricky time then, as we were a family living a Jewish life in a predominantly Christian era, and area. The remains of anti-Semitic stigma clung in the suburbs.

In accordance with tradition, I was given a Jewish symbol to wear, not a Star of David, but a gold heart engraved with the Hebrew word 'Mazal' (short for Mazal Tov – Good Luck) but the heart had to be worn pinned to my vest – I was not allowed to wear it on view on a chain round my neck.

(Interestingly, we have not moved on too far from this in a Christian sense, as it has been decreed by the Government that people do not have a legal right to wear a crucifix to work either. It seems that visible faith is still unacceptable, even in our enlightened society).

One of the great humiliations of my life was when I was expelled from the Scout movement girls' group, the Brownies, at the tender age of seven. I had trotted along with my friend Sue and enjoyed an introductory session … but when Mum filled in the forms, I was turned away for not being born into, or observant of, a Christian faith. I am sure these days the Brownies would not dare to be so exclusive, but in the early 1960s the decision was not opposed.

Aged eleven, I had an emergency hospital admission for a burst appendix at exactly the same time as the family moved home. By the time I was discharged we had relocated to a different part of Surrey, and I did not get a chance to say goodbye to my childhood home, school and friends. Further, being in hospital at the time, I missed the selection process for school admission following my passing the (then) eleven plus national exams.

Things were not terribly flexible in education at that time, and the only school my parents could get me into happened to be a local Roman Catholic Convent School.

Just imagine the confusion of an eleven-year-old pupil who called herself Jewish and had never been to church, being confronted with Christ on the cross on the wall in every room (even the toilets!) I also had to adjust to meeting a strong Catholic faith ethic and discipline, largely administered by teachers who were black-robed nuns.

As it turned out, I was quite happy at the all girls' school apart from being excluded from most assemblies, and of course the chapel for Mass. However, I remember once or twice creeping into the chapel, dipping my fingers in the small font by the door and guiltily crossing myself to see if anything would happen – it didn't.

One of the nuns, Sister Mary Magdalene, had the task of looking after we religious lepers (there were a couple of agnostics, so I was thankfully not alone in my exclusion) and I believe we passed our time in what was considered worthy reading at the time. But I was, in faith terms, very confused!

My mum was less entrenched in Judaism than dad. She was not born of Jewish parents, but her commitment to and love for my father led to her studying Judaism and correctly answering questions from the Chief Rabbi in order for her to be accepted into the faith, before they were married in a Synagogue.

For the family, Mum followed the observances of the Friday night Sabbath in providing a Kosher chicken for dinner most weeks; at that time, she had to travel by train in and out of London to buy the chickens from the Kosher butcher. But she always kept an open stance on religious matters and did not object to my theological musings, such as they were, during my formative years.

As a young adult, I did not follow any faith. It simply didn't have a place in my life, nor did I feel any need to follow a specific doctrine.

But when my children were young, I didn't want them to

feel excluded or different at school (as I had) and actively encouraged their taking part in the Christian festivals, so that they could share in the Harvest, Easter and nativity celebrations. I began to go to Sunday worship at our local church and I enjoyed the rhythm of it, but the services were rather stuffy and formal, so I never felt more than a sense of being part of something greater, though I suppose this was an achievement in itself.

Stella and James were baptised as young children and I have to thank my dad for being big-hearted enough to come to the church and even to hold a candle, despite it being against his religious principles.

Thus, I have always been somewhere on the religious fence. I wasn't really on the outside looking in. I was simply on the outside.

Since James died in 2005, I have often said, *"How I envy people who have a strong faith, something that sustains them through the darkest times of their lives."* Suddenly, through Alpha, I had the Damascene revelation that there is no reason why I, too, cannot have a faith. It is as accessible to me as it is to anyone else, even though I have not been born and brought up in the faith which I now choose to pursue.

Alpha made Christianity the most accessible and appealing belief system I have ever encountered.

My own epiphany arrived, and I didn't even know that I

had been searching for it!

At first, I felt really strange flipping the pages of the New Testament in the Bible to check references when the leader suggested we read a particular verse, appropriate to that point in the presentation. It was very new and different to be pursuing something that had been expressly forbidden by my father when I was young, but I was tremendously excited by the stories in this part of the Bible, which were all fresh to me.

Suddenly, I had this whole new vista opening up before me.

I was being guided to it in a safe place and a comfortable manner.

It was refreshingly different to anything I'd experienced.

One of the Alpha sessions was an entire day spent studying the Holy Spirit, to me the most nebulous and awe-inspiring element of the Holy Trinity. We travelled to a different church and there was a workshop atmosphere to the day. And on this day, I had a significant moment of revelation. The discussion turned to the supernatural and to the existence of angels. My ears pricked up.

I love the thought of angels, whether they are our guardian angels, angels with different attributes such as light, protection and healing, and so on. Suddenly, as I sat in a room at a church somewhere in suburbia, I learned that though I am a Christian, I do not have to give up my concurrent belief in the angelic realm.

This was an absolutely pivotal moment that continues to delight me.

I learned that angels are part of the Universe that God created. They are spiritual creatures and cannot usually be seen.

There are in fact only two angels named in the bible, the Archangel Michael and the angel Gabriel. Michael's title of Archangel indicates rule or authority over other angels. He is often invoked or prayed to in spiritual circles as a protector. He is depicted as a handsome, tall being wearing a cloak and I like the imagery that is associated with him.

I discovered too that even a dragon (aka the devil) turns up in the Bible, in the book of Revelation:[5]

'Then war broke out in heaven. Michael and his angels fought against the dragon, and the dragon and his angels fought back. But he was not strong enough, and they lost their place in heaven. The great dragon was hurled down—that ancient serpent called the devil, or Satan, who leads the whole world astray.'

And, it was the angel Gabriel who foretold the birth of Jesus in the book of Luke, when he visited Mary in Nazareth[6.]

But the angelic realm amounts to 'myriads, thousands' so we can be safe in the knowledge that there are enough to go around. I have always liked the idea of having a guardian angel and it seems that God sends angels for our protection. I loved reading in Psalm 91 the following affirmation of their role for us: [7]

'He will give his angels charge of you to guard you in all your ways. On their hands they will bear you up, lest you dash your foot against a stone.'

A belief in the existence of spiritual beings such as angels is a reminder to us that there is an unseen world that is as real as everything for which we have tangible, visible evidence.

The obverse side of the angelic realm is the existence of Satanic deception and the biblical origins cite Lucifer as the fallen angel who defied God. The dark arts act in direct opposition to angelic guidance.

I felt strangely inhibited about telling anyone I was doing the Alpha Course. Obviously, Shaun knew. He looked slightly bemused when I told him. *"What do you want to do that for?"* he asked me, puzzled.

I found it difficult to answer when I hadn't even started it and had no idea what to expect but I said, *'I just want to learn about something new. It doesn't mean I will turn into a regular churchgoer or anything ..."* (little did I know!)

My daughter Stella asked, *"Do you think it will help you to process what happened to James?"* And I think this was a very perspicacious question. I am always looking for things that can help me to process what happened to James.

During the Alpha course, I did not share my status of bereaved parent. In part it was because I knew that as soon as I shared that particular part of my story, the dynamic of the group would change.

There was, in fact, something curiously liberating about being with a new bunch of people and not having to be labelled with what had gone before.

I do think it is true to say that it coloured my contributions to our conversations. In particular, the 'Why me?' type of faith exploration questions which I answered, 'Why not me?' representing many hours of introspective examination of what has happened to me and its random nature. My newfound beliefs do indeed allow me to process what has happened, not just to James but also to my parents and my brother, in different and more profound ways.

I have become someone who is not afraid to ask, *"Would you like me to pray for you?"* or say: *"I will pray for you,"* to people when I know they are in difficult times.

C S Lewis says of Jesus[8],

'You must make your choice. Either this man was, or is, the son of God, or else he's a lunatic, or worse, the Devil of Hell. But don't let us come up with any patronising nonsense, about his being a great moral teacher. He hasn't left that open to us. He didn't intend to.'

It never occurred to me before, that religion could be

reduced to a simple choice. You can either believe, or not believe. There are no shades in between believing or not believing.

And it doesn't matter if you decide you believe now, tomorrow, or next week. Or if you have believed since you were old enough to formulate rational thoughts. To Christians, it appears that you are as welcome when you have just joined, as if you have always been part of the faith. And I love that sense of inclusion.

God loves me. Jesus loves me. The Holy Spirit loves me. Now I understand a little, tiny, scratching-the-surface part of these three facts. And am I uplifted and supported by them? Do they help me on a day to day level? Wow. Yes, they really do.

I acknowledge the presence of the Holy Spirit with an open mind.

And find that I can now utilise my learning of the Christian faith and use it to help me process my grief. But further than that, I feel uplifted, comforted and supported in a way that simply was not there before.

I always thought that the term *born again Christian* was modern, but according to the Gospel of John, Jesus says to one of the Pharisees[9], *"Very truly I tell you, no one can see the kingdom of God unless they are **born again**."* I guess that the full panoply of being born again includes baptism, but according to Alpha I became a Christian the moment I decided that I believe in the faith. That's good enough for me at the moment. In fact, I prefer to call myself a new Christian, and I also love the idea that by joining the faith, I am truly a daughter of God.

I have a better understanding that there can be a cross over from Christian faith and doctrine and other forms of healing work … as a spiritual healer once said to me, *"All healing is simply God's love for us."*

Many of us deny the reality of anything we cannot see. But do we deny the wind that blows in the trees? Do we deny the sound of a distant wave on the ocean, heard long before we see it? Do we deny our own emotions and thoughts, our intuition?

If you are outside on a windy day you have a good allegory for faith.

It has many and varied attributes:

You can feel the wind, but you cannot see or grasp it.

You cannot tell where it comes from or where it is going.

You can see what it does, but you cannot affect or influence its behaviour.

You can hear it softly rustling in the trees or loudly gusting.

You can be stung by its cold bite or cooled by its gentle caress.

You can smell in the air a drift of autumn wood smoke or

summer flowers

You can resist it or accept it, but you cannot change it.

You can see it as a wonder, or maybe a curse.

You need to believe in it because its evidence is irrefutable.

The wind also behaves like the passage of grief – and how it is in the beginning when you feel as though you are spinning helplessly in the vortex of a tornado, tumbled in a chaotic maelstrom of shock and loss. You are buffeted this way and that, tossed heedlessly by this monstrous unfamiliar blast. And then … gradually, the storm begins to lose power.

The strength of it recedes. Its violence becomes spent through hours, days, weeks of working through your tears and sorrow, until the havoc of storm force drops back to an acceptable level that your poor bruised heart, mind and soul can accommodate.

You reach a point where the howling tempest of the early days can be consigned to memory. You know that your face has lost the windswept, bewildered look of early loss and that you have come through the fierceness of the storm and out the other side. Where before all you could see was cloud and darkness, now you can appreciate the sunshine and rainbows again. These experiences with the natural world are akin to faith.

When you are locked into the despair of grief, you cry out

for help and you do not know where that help is coming from, but you have faith that it *will* come, and it *will* help you.

You cannot see faith, and you might believe you live without it, but as time passes, perhaps you recognise that faith is helping to give you strength to get through the difficulties in life.

Faith is trusting what you cannot see.

Faith is like taking a walk in the dark and believing you will not trip over unseen obstacles. Faith is reaching out and knowing you will not be ignored or knocked back.

Faith is trusting in your own beliefs without constantly seeking logical evidence.

Faith is living comfortably with mystery.

The wind and faith share the intangibility of a concept that has no beginning, and no end. How often do you do something that you describe as *a leap of faith* when you step forward into the unfamiliar, safe in the knowledge that you will be supported and encouraged? Sometimes you underestimate how much your faith and self-belief can uplift, nourish and sustain you. It is not really blind faith at all.

I wrote about wind and faith some time before I encountered the following words in the Bible from the Gospel of John:[10]

'Flesh gives birth to flesh, but the Spirit gives birth to spirit. You should not be surprised at my saying, 'You must be born again.' The wind blows wherever it pleases. You hear its sound, but you cannot tell where it comes from or where it is going. So it is with everyone born of the Spirit.'

I was amazed at how closely my thoughts mirrored the words of Jesus as written by John, especially as I had not read them before.

I have no idea what James would think of my conversion to faith. Despite my efforts to produce conforming Christian children, neither Stella nor James showed much interest in faith once they reached their teens. They both studied religious education at school, but I don't recall that there were any in depth discussions at home about their beliefs. I think that for many people it is not until they reach adulthood, and perhaps have a family themselves, that faith becomes an issue worthy of serious consideration.

So, out of the patchwork beliefs of my childhood, today I stand proudly embracing Christianity. It definitely is one of those *who would have thought it?* concepts for me.

The situation was totally different in 2001, when any faith that I had was utterly rocked by the death of my mum. I felt then that my feeble incursions into being godly had never been enough, and I certainly did not feel that faith could sustain me. When James died, I sought solace in other spiritual and faith paths. I was angry with God. My perception was that He had taken away those precious people and all I could see was the unfairness of this.

I had no idea how to process my feelings, and I was not drawn to faith for the answers, if indeed they existed for me. I was wary of getting into what I saw as the formality of Church, not realising just how much faith observance has moved on in the intervening years – after all it was the best part of 30 years since my active involvement in church. It was certainly not my first choice for spiritual sustenance.

When you are living with loss, you can simply feel that everyday life is just too overwhelming at times. It is common to feel that there aren't enough hours in the day to fit everything in.

Instead of doing a few things well, you try to do too many things and the end result is a panicky feeling of not being able to achieve anything properly.

This is where, for me, faith began to come in through the door. I knew that I was looking for something to focus on that would bring me a measure of serenity. In the ancient rhythm of exploring faith: contemplation, prayer, getting to know God, I have begun to achieve it.

When tragedy strikes in life, there is a need to find places of refuge and spiritual solace.

In my own experience, when I look back across my

searches for spiritual sustenance, I see an evolution of my beliefs and my exploration of faith as something that steadily grows more meaningful and supportive.

Faith offers profound opportunities to get to know yourself better, and to learn that you are not alone. Faith teaches that God's hand is holding you whatever you do and wherever you go. This simple truth elates me daily.

In loss, we identify with the suffering of Jesus. In loss as a bereaved parent, surely, I might identify with God as he himself knows what it is to feel the agony of a bereaved parent. Or is that too fanciful, if not arrogant? We see weakness and travail becoming strength repeatedly in the Bible and if we were always strong, never showing signs of weakness, we would not need the lessons of faith to teach us how to move forward. Trusting in faith adds a new dimension to the travails of grief, lessening their impact and helping the processing of the emotions surrounding them.

Healing does not necessarily mean making you completely better. Healing means getting you to a place where you can live with your grief or loss. And faith plays an important part in the process of reaching that place.

I used to think that if you were a Christian, to tick all God's boxes in what is desirable in a person of religious faith, you had to go to church on Sundays, know the Bible intimately, be of sober and generous disposition and pray a lot. Then, I figured you would have this kind of hotline to God and Jesus that would sustain you in times of trouble and emphasise your joys.

I felt that these fortunate, faithful Christian people of my imagining were somehow more than I was, somehow better, because they had clear vision of their faith and this in turn produced a neat framework for their lives.

How wrong was I! My naivety was in fact quite staggering because I felt that faith was denied to me. It couldn't be mine because I hadn't been born to it and as old as I am, even as a mature adult, I was still seeking my parents' approval for my incursion into this unknown area. Alpha made all the foregoing reservations disappear as though they never existed. I agree with Bear Grylls when he says[11],

"At the heart of Christianity is the belief that we are loved and held and forgiven, and I try not to complicate my faith beyond that."

I feel that I needed to be given permission to access the Christian faith, and I believe that permission has come directly not from my father, but from The Father, God himself.

The clarity of my new belief which feels as though it shines like a beacon from me the majority of the time must surely come from the fact that the Holy Spirit has come to reside in my heart, along with those whom I have loved and lost, and those whom I love who are here today.

I found it difficult to understand the concept of Father, Son and Holy Spirit being three in one until I was given this description. An Alpha leader said, *"As a scientist, I can see water, ice and steam are three entirely different manifestations of the same thing ... so it is with God the Father, God the Son and God the Holy Spirit."* Even more impressively, they manage to be these three things at the same time, which is too far beyond our thinking to grasp but it is a profound and illustrative analogy that really works.

After the Alpha course ended, I was surprised to find that I genuinely wanted to continue attending church on a Sunday. Christchurch in Woking is a large town church with a congregation that spans every age range and represents the diverse local population.

It's a busy church with lively services and interesting sermons – these are less sermon and more informative talk.

I thoroughly enjoyed my attendances which were only halted by our move to Devon, some 150 miles away. Singing, worshipping and communal praying – all new to me and all so enjoyable.

When we moved to Bampton, I decide not to attend the small village church as I was anxious not to stand out as a new worshipper in a smaller congregation.

Needing the comfort of something familiar, I sought out one of the town churches in Tiverton. I was made extremely welcome the moment I walked through the door. The vicar, Andy, often reminds us as a congregation of our individual gifts. He says, *"God gives you all gifts to help you realise your potential in life."* And I believe that God has given me the gift to see and live in the mourning light. His light is in me, and it became clear only after I had embraced the truly dreadful darkness of losing James.

People might say, *"How can you believe in a God who allows dreadful things to happen?"* As I have previously mentioned, I asked that myself when my lovely mum suffered dreadfully before she died, and at that time I certainly turned away from faith because I believed it was unfairly weighted. But over time I have come to understand that we cannot always know and understand the reasons why something awful has happened to us. There is no good answer to that question.

Today, my belief in God, Jesus and the Holy Spirit is lighting my life in a way that nothing else has. I formerly thought that churchgoers were a bit smug, as if they were specially chosen to live that type of life. I know now that we all have the capacity to be part of that chosen group; and we aren't smug!

People who practise their faith, whatever form it takes,

may well be different. They shine out a soul light, which brings such great joy. When I am part of the worshipping congregation on a Sunday, through song and prayer, I always feel uplifted, supported and tremendously grateful for what faith is bringing to my life. I want to praise and thank God all the time for what he is doing for me. I am no longer a bad weather pray-er, just asking for his help when I am in a dark place, nor am I any longer a plea-bargaining pray-er *"Please God, if you just do so and so I will give up so and so ..."* Now I pray because I want to have conversations with God. Does he speak back? Well, I can't claim to have had any miraculous experiences, but I think my faith is making me a better-rounded person. I believe another gift in my faith is to bring help and understanding of grief to others who are struggling with loss.

There is a 'can do' attitude to modern Christianity which promises that simply by believing and having faith you will be stronger and better placed to face life's obstacles.

First Christchurch and now St George's and St Paul's have welcomed me with an unconditional warmth that has asked nothing from me in return.

If I was asked to sum up my feeling about church itself, I could describe it in one word – welcoming. There's no agenda, no insistence on attendance, no raised eyebrow if I miss a few weeks. The genuine caring attitude of all the people whom I have met since my Alpha revelations is very precious.

Whatever my faith path, wherever my faith journey has taken me, it has always been with conviction that there is something more awaiting me after this lifetime and my Christian learning simply serves to reinforce this in the most uplifting, hopeful ways possible.

Christ's life, death and resurrection each demonstrate the strength, power and commitment of a religion that does not simply talk the talk to its disciples, but walks the walk of a life that is made less burdensome by a belief in the unseen strength and support of an undemanding, ever present form of love. Faith love is entirely unconditional, asking nothing more than simple belief. The support network of the Christian church that I have encountered offers a welcoming embrace. Its message is simple and unassuming ... *"come one, come all"* and it is here to help us all on our spiritual journey without either question or judgement on what may have gone before.

The inner joy that has become mine with the acceptance of faith and all that it represents is an innate thing.

It is different to mere pleasure that is the result of external stimuli – it is a heartfelt, mind/body/spirit delight that is sustaining and wonderful. I like balance and rhythm in my life, and there is a rhythm to faith that follows the cycle of the year with a pleasing sense of order and symmetry to it. The rites and rituals of faith are, to my mind, undemanding. They do not impose upon me a strict regime that calls for my presence in Church on a Sunday, although I have been very pleased to find that this does not feel like a chore, but like a choice. When I joined the Alpha course, I truly took a leap – not of faith, but to faith. I jumped into hitherto unexplored territory with my eyes wide open and my mind receptive to whatever was on offer.

The excitement of discovering a whole new arena of spiritual wisdom, teaching, nurturing, sustenance is extreme, and it is honestly adding an enormous dimension to my being.

The poem, *Footprints in the Sand*, by Mary Stevenson[12] sums up my feelings about faith very well.

'One night I dreamed I was walking along the beach with the Lord. Many scenes from my life flashed across the sky.

In each scene I noticed footprints in the sand. Sometimes there were two sets of footprints, other times there was one only.

This bothered me because I noticed that during the low periods of my life, when I was suffering from anguish, sorrow or defeat, I could see only one set of footprints, so I said to the Lord,

"You promised me Lord, that if I followed you, you would walk with me always.

But I have noticed that during the most trying periods of my life there has only been one set of footprints in the sand. Why, when I needed you most, have you not been there for me?"

The Lord replied, "The years when you have seen only one set of footprints, my child, is when I carried you.'

Chapter 6

And Love Endures

Touched by an Angel

We, unaccustomed to courage
Exiles from delight
Live coiled in shells of loneliness
Until love leaves its high holy temple
and comes into our sight
To liberate us into life.

Love arrives
and in its train come ecstasies
Old memories of pleasure
Ancient histories of pain
Yet if we are bold,
Love strikes away the chains of fear
from our souls.

We are weaned from our timidity
in the flush of love's light
We dare to be brave
and suddenly we see
That love costs all we are
And will ever be
Yet it is only love
which sets us free.

This poem by Maya Angelou[1] provides beautiful reflections about the innate attribute which we all possess, that 'crazy

137

little thing called love.'

Apparently, the question most frequently asked on Google is *"What is love?"*

It is such a nebulous concept that no-one has ever been able to give it a single, definitive descriptor. I guess it is as individual as we are ourselves. Its commonality is that all love comes from the heart. We cannot force it or make it be there, it is intrinsic to our makeup.

Some of us have more than others.

Some of us abuse it, but most of us embrace it and hold it dear, affording it the status it deserves throughout our lives.

If hope stands in a corner with both feet planted firmly on the ground, and if light shines out from within so that you bring others into your beam, then love encompasses all the emotion you ever feel, whether that is touched by joy or sadness.

A while ago, I received an email from Linda Cook, a former colleague and friend, asking if I could send her a few loving words describing her mum Madeleine (also a friend) as she was making her a word cloud that she planned to print out and frame to give to Madeleine as a gift.

"What is a word cloud?" I asked Linda, and she directed me to the Wordle website[2].

Basically, Wordle is an app for generating patterns, called word clouds, from your text. You can tweak your clouds with different fonts, layouts, and colour schemes.

The images you create with Wordle are yours to use however you like. You can print them out or save them to the Wordle gallery to share with your friends.

I duly sent some words to Linda and then I idled away some time on Wordle myself. I created two word clouds, one comprising negative words such as fear and anxiety, and one positive, for example sunshine and light, reflecting how I view the progression of my own grief since James died.

I printed out the word clouds and when I studied them, I noticed there was a single word that appeared in both of the lists, the positive and the negative. And that word is... love.

Is love, then, one of the most important keys to grieving? Perhaps it is. Because it is love for your lost child, parent, sibling, peer, friend, colleague, neighbour, that is the first and foremost emotion surrounding their passing.

It is love that fuels your compassion and empathy.

It is love which gives you the ability to feel both pain and pleasure.

It is love which allows you to feel the greatest joy and the utmost sadness.

It is the love which you shared with the person who died that populates your memories of them and it is love that ensures your grief gradually becomes a gentler thing.

It may seem odd to talk of love when you think of the rage, fear and tumult of early loss ... but the love that you feel coming back at you from those around you - when you are ready - is an extremely important part of the grieving process.

Grief and loss and love are, it seems to me, inextricably bound up together and I am thankful for that. And for all the reading and writing there is to teach us about love, I relate to this quote by the founder of the Methodist movement, John Wesley, who said:[3]

"Beware you be not swallowed up in books! An ounce of love is worth a pound of knowledge."

You don't have to think about love. There is no need to consider it, or measure it, embrace it, reject it or put it aside. Love in its many forms exists as an entity in itself.

There are four ancient words for love that are particularly used in faith terms: agape, eros, phileo and storge.

Agape, (pronounced Ah-gah-pay) is a particular kind of love, and when you read a little more about it, you can decide whether or not you walk with agape.

One definition of agape, which comes from Greek, is 'unconditional love that is always giving and impossible to take.'

It devotes total commitment to seeking your highest best no matter how anyone may respond. This form of love is totally selfless and does not change whether the love given is returned, or not.

That is a tall order for mere humans! - we naturally tend to measure our giving and receiving love, and ego may tell us that we are the best judges of whether we should give our love or not. But a key principle of agape love is that is not about mutual point scoring, it is freely given without anticipation of return. Agape can be viewed as the highest form of love, and it encompasses the best of brotherly love and charity. It is further described as the love of God for man and of man for God, to illustrate something of its selfless and giving nature.

In his book *Resilient*, (cited in Chapter 5) author Sheridan Voysey sums up his view of agape when he writes,

"Good relationships are intrinsically mutual, and business should be fair— reciprocity has its place. But in my darkest, weakest, most fruitless moments I need agape.

And with God's strength, I want to give it. Beyond business deals and mutual friendship, I want to give without requiring anything in return."

Dogs are a good example of agape love. Whether they are ignored or pampered, they wag their tails and greet us with affection. The beginning of each day is an especially happy time for dogs.

They bring no baggage with them from the day before and this is an example that we would do well to follow. They give unconditially, and do not differentiate between getting either a scolding or a stroke in return. They are entirely unaffected by our response to their agape; they just keep on giving regardless. They are entirely without resentment.

We feel agape love for our children from the moment they are born and as a mother who has lost her son, I still feel agape love for James; a form of love that will remain unchanged and undiminished for the rest of my life.

And maybe it is agape love that keeps his memories so strong in my heart; he is with me for every beat.

I like the saying, *"Yesterday is history, tomorrow is a mystery, but today is a gift,"* for we have no idea what each day will bring. That seems to me to sit well with the principles of agape love which has a purity of spirit about it that neither grasps nor demands.

It is agape love that draws us to acts of charity, when we are sensitive to the needs of others, we may be practising a degree of agape without even realising it.

There are numerous descriptions of agape love:

Agape love is strong, powerful and forgiving.

Agape is the love that is shared in robust relationships that have gone past the heady days of trying to impress.

Agape loves in such ways that it makes us feel cherished and beautiful.

Agape is based upon giving through sharing and understanding that when you share, you are not losing anything, but you are gaining.

Agape love transcends the concept of needing to be forgiven

To even scratch at the surface of the concept of agape love I begin to see that it is necessary to set aside the rules that we accept as the norm in our philosophical loving relationships: by this I mean that we generally measure love in give and take terms.

Thus, we limit ourselves in our capacity for agape love as these terms do not apply in a love which is both sharing and unconditional.

It should be easy to define something that is totally without demands or requirements, but it is not!

Theologian William, Barclay, noted:[4] *"Agape has to do with the mind: it is not simply an emotion which rises unbidden in our hearts; it is a principle by which we deliberately live. Further, it is a form of love that is related to obedience and commitment, not necessarily feeling and emotion."*

So there we have it. Agape is a highly selfless form of love, it is a principle, it is an overwhelming, elusive something that we should aspire to if we can grasp its concepts. Perhaps this is something to grapple with in your quiet moments. Give yourself some thinking time and open your heart to feel the agape.

Eros love is important to mention because it represents the undeniably heady flame of attraction in love. Eros is personified by the Greek god of love. This is not the forum for discussion of erotic love; suffice to say that most of us will be lucky enough to have a visitation from Eros at some point in our lives.

The meaning of phileo love is initially quite hard to grasp. It is described as a love that has 'a special interest in someone or something, frequently with focus on close association; have affection for, like, consider someone a friend.' With that description, I can think of various people for whom I feel this type of emotion, though it is not as deep or clear cut as love. Rather it is perhaps closer to the companionship that I share with friends of longstanding.

You know that feeling: when you have not seen a friend for some time, and you meet. You immediately pick up where you left off last time. To me, that illustrates phileo love.

Storge, a word which I had never encountered before I began to examine forms of love for my writing, is the love and affection that naturally occurs between parents and children, can exist between siblings, and exists between husband and wife in a good marriage. The comfort of this very specific type of love when you are grieving cannot be overestimated. After losing James, I would have found my life far more difficult without the *storge* I am lucky to have around me.

As well as the love I share with my husband, this family storge love and affection extends to my daughter, stepchildren, their partners and my grandchildren, and the growth of such love is soothing balm to the process of grieving.

Hope is one of three great theological virtues – the others being love and faith. As Raniero Cantalamessa writes:[5] *"They are like three sisters. Two of them are grown and the other is a small child. They go forward together hand in hand with the child hope in the middle. Looking at them it would seem that the bigger ones are pulling the child, but it is the other way around; it is the little girl who is pulling the two bigger ones. It is hope that pulls faith and love. Without hope, everything would stop."*

Similarly, if hope, light and faith are the ingredients, then love is the binding agent in this strange recipe for working through your grief and mourning.

Hope, light and faith are intrinsically linked, but they are nothing without the thing that underpins them, and that is love. There is no greater unconditional love than that which we feel for our children. From the moment of birth and even before, as mothers, and fathers, we love the precious miracle of the person we are carrying and bringing into the world. All our hopes for the future are contained in our offspring, and when their lives are cruelly cut short, it is truly devastating.

Bereaved mother, Jackie Ford-Low lost her precious son Owen in 2012. He drowned in a swimming pool accident in Ibiza on his first holiday abroad. Since his accident, Jackie has worked tirelessly to fundraise for drowning prevention in the area where she lives in Scotland. I know that like all mums of lost children, she struggles to work through her grief and loss.

Four years on, Jackie wrote from the heart:

"I miss him.

I miss his smell,

I miss his laugh,

I miss his cheek,

I miss the smell of Lynx in the house,

I miss him coming home on a Friday with a football coupon, insisting I fill it out,

I miss his music,

I miss the phone ringing, the door knocking for him,

I miss him winding the dog up,

I miss him winding me up,

I miss him asking 'What's for tea?'

I miss everything there is to miss about him.

I look at his brothers and his pals ... they are no longer teenagers and boys now, but they are men and I miss the future that Owen has been denied.

I look back at the photos of the boys as babies....as young boys...at primary school....at High School and I miss those days.

My complete family in one photo. I miss the easiness of it all then ... never ever did I ever think we would lose Owen.

I just bloody miss him."

Over the years of my membership of TCF I have met a number of other bereaved parents. Linda Sewell introduced me to Sarah O'Donoghue, who does a great deal of voluntary work for the charity and who has run a local support group for some years. She also travels extensively in the UK, training other TCF volunteers in how to set up and facilitate groups.

I knew that Sarah would make a valuable contribution to any discussion about how love endures after child loss and we met for a coffee and chat on a particularly grey February morning.

Sarah told me what happened to her son, Charlie.

"It was 2003. Charlie was out in Kingston celebrating his 'A' level results with friends and at the end of the evening he should simply have come home on the train. Instead of that, the first we knew anything was wrong was when the police turned up the following day with the awful news that he had fallen and been found on the railway line."

Sarah and I talked for a while about how the immense, traumatic shock of such accidents affects us as parents. We are hopeful that there will be a diminution in such incidents in the future as advances in technology mean it is much easier for groups to keep in contact with each other when they are out socialising.

Ideally this means that in future, the circumstances that are familiar to both Sarah and I, along with many other families who have lost teenagers to accident, will be less likely to arise.

Sarah shared with me that about six months after Charlie's death she had been diagnosed with post-traumatic stress disorder. She described an example of a specialist cognitive tool that may be helpful to others in similar, distressing circumstances. She told me:

"One of the worst things was that I couldn't stop my mind repeatedly seeing images of Charlie lying there on the track. I was taught to replace the images, so that instead of seeing him lying there, I saw him getting up and walking towards me. Initially the counsellor suggested I saw him getting up and walking away, but for me, it worked to see him coming towards me. After all, how could it be comforting to see him walking away?"

This concept makes total sense to me and echoes my own practice of visualising James well, happy and enjoying life. None of us want to imagine our children being anything other than that.

I would reiterate what I have said before; that all parents suffer from post-traumatic stress to some degree after the loss of a child, and this is often insufficiently recognised and treated. Many of us find we need to muddle through by ourselves, as best we can.

We suffer a form of emotional death with the loss of our children, and we have to find ways of coming back from that. We have to build new dreams for a future that does not include them in our families, and we need to re-engage with life. This takes time, but it is achievable.

Sarah's motives for supporting others after loss are admirably altruistic. She said:

"I do what I do for TCF because it is good to see people return to relatively normal functioning after something so awful ... the ideal, I think, is for people to join the group, come along, and use the group to help them work through what has happened.

They know they are in a safe, supportive, non-judgemental setting where there is an emphasis on processing positively, to get them through the worst of times."

She went on to say: *"It is not always possible for everyone to get to this point, it doesn't happen if it is not right for them but I always encourage the ultimate aim – that is for your grief to stop being all of who you are, and to become part of who you are."*

I consider this a very profound truth.

The evolution of grief eventually allows it to become a

piece of the jigsaw rather than the whole puzzle.

Like many people, Sarah had occasions where she was frustrated by how little her grief and loss were understood by others. She was told on occasion: *"You should be over it by now,"* *"You need to stop crying every day."* - both crass and insensitive statements.

She also said that when she went to see her GP after Charlie died, he looked at her in the way we both recognise as the 'cloying sympathy' look, and said to her *"Poor you,"* which was hardly what she needed at the time.

We agreed that what we need early on are people who could tell us with authority that it can get easier to bear, and the agony will lessen in time.

I asked Sarah how her husband Tony and her other children, Sophie and Edward, cope with having lost their son and brother.

"I found it hard at first, always thinking that they would need to talk, when in fact it was impossible to force them to and gradually, I accepted that they had to work it out in their own way." Sarah realises that family members are sometimes too close to each other to be able to help and share their grief. Everyone in the situation is grieving and therefore it behoves each individual to look for help outside the immediate circle, (always assuming that they want and need to).

We touched on the difference in the way that women and

men grieve, too. Sarah said: *"It's common for husbands and wives to have times when they turn outwards and away from each other in their grief, rather than inwards."*

We agree that men and women grieve entirely differently, women needing to talk – usually a great deal – whereas most men process loss without an apparent need to discuss their emotions. Whilst I accept this is a rather sweeping generalisation, it is a commonly observed phenomenon in grief and loss circles.

In real terms, processing the loss of our children, for women, comes down to a simple fact. As Sarah observed: *"It's a bit like giving birth. No-one else can do it for you. You've got to do all the pushing yourself."* Such a true statement!

Sarah is now 16 years post loss and she says she has now realised she is at a point where she needs to step back from the intensity of grieving. *"I would say,"* she told me, *"that the healing is there, but it's still a wound. I need to recognise the value of looking after myself, being kind to myself and not giving out all the time."*

Supporting others who are grieving is hard, sustained work and I understand Sarah's saying that *"you can't pour from an empty vessel."* We who work with grief and loss, be it privately or publicly, need to make sure we conserve our own energies and don't give too much of ourselves. To do so hinders our own progress on the road to the ultimate assimilation of our loss.

151

A while ago, I heard Sarah say that during sessions her well-meaning grief counsellor tried to get her to 'leave her son behind.' Like me, Sarah feels that her son comes with her, is part of her and is with her every day. I wholly agree with her when she says, *"He's not here to live his life; I am. And I owe it to him and to myself to enjoy life."*

Perhaps only other bereaved parents can fully understand that our children remain part of our lives and even though their lives with us are over, yet they remain as part of our present and indeed our future, to enable us to balance out our grieving whilst continuing to live meaningfully. Our grief evolves over time so that is not as desperate as it was early on, and it is a great relief to arrive at this more comfortable place. At the outset, we need to hear from others that there is hope of achieving a balanced existence again. This requires the greatest love of all, the love that a parent has for his or her child, and also resilience, about which Sarah says,

"Resilience is remembering it's a marathon, not a sprint."

I see in Sarah innate strength, warmth and a genuine desire to help others through the difficulties of adapting to life as bereaved parents. Her generously given contribution is considerable and I am sure her efforts are appreciated by all the families with whom she comes into contact.

There are many things that I love about my late Mum,

gone from us now for more than a decade. Firstly, she was an excellent, intuitive cook.

And she warmly welcomed my friends over the years, often plying them with meals which were prepared with much love and affection.

In fact, she was a cook ahead of her time, as she produced spaghetti bolognaise – with fresh garlic – in the 1960s, when such *foreign food* was viewed as strange and exotic. I remember too, on hot summer days, she made wonderfully tasty Spanish gazpacho – a chilled soup with a tomato base into which was added garlicky bread soaked in a little olive oil, the whole being enhanced with finely chopped peppers and cucumber. Delicious! And watching Mum make a Victoria sponge or bake an apple pie was an education in itself. She didn't weigh or measure the ingredient but said she could tell the balance was right "*by feel.*" Somehow her sponges always turned out light and airy; her pastry was invariably short and crisp.

Mum had some favourite recipes and she was happy to share them. So it was that her ratatouille recipe (which owes little to a traditional ratatouille as she did not like the flavour of aubergines/eggplant) found its way to the recipe file belonging to Stella, one of my friends from school days.

Recently Stella, who has lived in the US for many years

with her American husband, mentioned that she often cooked mum's ratatouille to serve as a side dish with roast chicken and I realised that I did not have the recipe. She kindly scanned and emailed it to me.

There is something very special about seeing the handwriting of someone you love after they have passed. Mum's writing is distinctive, with cursive script, large capitals and extravagant loops and swirls. It is not dull writing but has a liveliness of form. The phrasing of Mum's ratatouille recipe brings her to mind in a lovely way. I can almost hear her as she describes the method. In particular I can picture her expression and her hand movements as she suggests *'swizzling the oil.'* I especially like the instruction to *'cover with foil and plonk lid on top'* – very emphatic.

Over the long years of our friendship, my late friend Sylvi also met my parents and when I visited her at her home in France in 2015, we talked of my mum. *"I've still got your mum's fruit cake recipe,"* she told me. It's another one that I didn't have. Soon afterwards the recipe arrived in the post and once again, I could conjure up something of Mum's character from the writing and composition.

Her recipes owe little to a formulaic list of ingredients and processes; they are somehow far more personal. I love her comment about sugar in the recipe: *"4 1/2ozs is enough unless you have a very sweet tooth"* which reflects mum's personal preference too. Equally, her clarification of how to avoid the cherries sinking to the bottom of the mixture *("Push them into the cake batter at the end, just half an inch or so down")* personalises the recipe in a way that would not be found in a book. Her exhortation at the end of the recipe to enjoy *happy baking!* is typical of Mum's desire to please others.

The exchange of recipes today is far more likely to happen electronically, and it is the work of an instant to share a recipe with many; Mum's distribution was undoubtedly more selective and perhaps has added value for that. I wonder how many more of her recipes there are hidden away in people's files.

Handwriting is as unique as a voice or a fingerprint and there are certain characteristics specific to the way Mum wrote things down which are personal to her. Interestingly, when she wrote a shopping list, she used the whole sheet (usually the back of an envelope).

Rather than writing a sequential list, she would dot words all around the space in seemingly random order. I have never thought about why I do it, but I find I do exactly the same. Mum's writing never varied much; her hand was always neat and decisive. She wrote to me often, invariably heading up her letters with a humorous take on her address, such as *"Sunny Vista"* on a dull winter's day or *"Shady Nook"* in midsummer, and she always closed with

"Ever your loving mum," indeed she was that, and still is.

There is an intimacy and individuality to handwriting that does not exist in the typed word, however emotive or personal the topic. Handwriting reflects us in a way that is entirely unique. We develop a writing style and voice that expresses our own identity.

I still enjoy writing personal letters, notes and cards as an adjunct to electronic communication. Sadly, the pleasure of handwriting is under-emphasised in today's world and it would be a pity if this individual skill were to be lost altogether.

I do not need the skills of a graphologist to know that Mum's handwriting echoes her merry personality and exuberance for life and the evidence, in the form of her recipes if nothing else, is indeed precious to keep.

The love I still feel for my mother, even though she has been gone for many years now, is undimmed by time. The memories are not as clear as they once were, but it still takes very little for me to be able to conjure her up in my mind. There is so much she has missed, but I still feel she is part of my life from the wisdom she passed down to me. I like to think that I possess some of my mum's qualities built into my DNA. She was warm and kind and I hope that I am too. I miss her guidance, her humour but most of all I miss being able to chat easily with her.

The love I feel for my mum and for my friend are two different levels, or types, of love, but they both reflect how different aspects of this emotion are shared in so many different ways: through face to face contact, photographs and handwriting.

Author and psychotherapist Annie Broadbent, whom I met in 2014 at the launch of her excellent and supportive bereavement book *Speaking of Death: What the Bereaved Really Need*[5] has a refreshing attitude towards talking about the loss of those whom we love.

Annie shared her story and the stories of others to give some guidelines on how best to support someone grieving for a loved one. In itself, her book demonstrates a truly loving act from a daughter to a mother and it touches a chord with every reader. Annie continues to write movingly following the loss of a mother who was clearly so pivotal in her life.

Using the device of letters, she brings to life the conversations that she has with her mother. Annie is young; she was very unfortunate to lose her mum when she was only 25 and the milestones of her life as she lives on without her are poignant.

April 2015

Hi mama

I'm so sorry I've been putting this off. It still amazes me how painful it is to write to you. I'm sitting here with Tim, my fiancé! How cool is that?! I'm getting married! To that guy! That guy I told you about years ago. It breaks my heart that you never got to meet him – I think you'd probably both end up spending more time together than I would with either of you. Honestly Mum, you would adore him.

And we'd all have such nice times the three of us – it's so real in my head, as though it's a memory. I can't believe I have to do this without you – I feel like only you would know the answer to so many things – or only your answer would do, like the bloody guest list?! Who should I invite?! And who can I not bother with?

Ahh, the wave has washed away for now – it was too much. They have come and gone ever since you died; huge waves of pain, that drown you entirely, and then drain away as quickly as they come.

Now I've started this letter, I don't really want to stop. A part of me knows that once I've written this then I need to proceed, move on with being engaged and getting married. And yet … I can't, because I feel on another level that by getting married without you, I am abandoning you.

It also feels so much like having a conversation with you. I know that's why I'm probably not going into detail yet about the whole experience – the fairy-tale proposal, our life together, our plans – it's as though by telling you I have to confront a feeling of betrayal – because it's acknowledging having kept it from you all this time.

I taught him 'soup to nuts' - the way you would want to know every detail of my experiences, from start to finish. If ever I'd skim over something you'd say 'soup to nuts please.' It's one of the things I miss the most about you - not *feeling that level of interest you had in me from anyone else. But I feel it with him! I feel safe and invited to tell him all the details of my experiences in life and we have such amazing conversations.*

He's going to write to you as well – to tell you his story. He will tell you a beautiful story, in his beautiful way. He's taught me so much – I feel a bit shy about telling this to you because I think he'll probably read this letter, but I think the most important thing is he's taught me how to accept love. I can't tell you how hard it was at the beginning – and we had some rocky times too – but we really worked through them. We have so much fun together Mum. He taught me how to play.

May 2015

Mutti – I went wedding dress shopping today! Kari came with me and was so lovely. It was surreal – I so desperately wanted to walk out of the changing room and see your face gasp at the dress I was wearing – or turn your nose up – I feel like I can't make decisions again. Everything feels so difficult. And I hate not really knowing what you'd like. Which dress did you prefer? Please tell me.

You would have so loved hearing about the proposal – and I would have enjoyed telling you about it almost as much as experiencing it – I would have rung you first and you would have screamed down the phone 'Yippeeeeeeeee!"

You would have burst in to tears and I would have missed you, and been so excited to see you and dance around – and you would have got a folder out and got busy and I would feel so safe in the knowledge that you were all for me – that I was your Number One girl, that there were no limits, that I had someone there who cared for me more than anyone else in the world.

Oh let me tell you about the proposal. Christmas morning, 7am. I woke up to him drawing me in for a cuddle and saying to me "Good morning, love of my life." I gave him some presents and he nearly cried at my photo frame with the quote 'Set me like a seal upon thy heart, love is as strong as death.' Then he said my present was outside. The truth is, I had been having these obsessive thoughts about him proposing but honestly never in a million years actually believed he was planning it – I know how much he likes to make an effort about lots of things, and so I thought he would go to a lot of lengths just to present me with a present. I was trying to convince myself it was a bike. He seemed so excited, like a little boy – putting on his turquoise pants (to go with the Tiffany box!) and then we ran across the lawn.

It's weird how normal it will be not to have you there at the wedding, and yet it is not normal. And the truth is, it will be a little bit less without you Mama. I will feel a little bit more alone. I will feel the absence of my Number One team mate.

July 2015

I try not to do it but it feels impossible not to compare every activity with how it would be if you were there. There is no-one in the world I trust more than you – so I feel the whole burden of decision for everything on me – and Tim of course. I already messed up because you're not here by inviting nearly everyone in the world – obviously trying to compensate for the pain of not being able to tell you.

I can't believe you had to die – you were so incredibly cool – and you really knew how to live life and do great things – it's so unfair. And now I really want to know what it was like – I can't believe you had to go through that

alone – you were so unbelievably brave – never once telling us you were afraid.
I so desperately want to hear your voice – and see a video of you – I wish we'd
done that – for these later years. Nearly four now. I can't believe it.
September – 3 weeks before
Well, things have really stepped up a gear mum. And I miss you so much.
I realised the other day that I'm really scared. I don't remember feeling that
since you died – feeling scared of what I'm about to do because you're not
here. But this is the biggest thing – without you I feel like I'm walking in
foggy terrain. I've also realised how hard I'm finding it to validate myself
without you – I'm being quite hard on myself and feel like I'm making lots
of mistakes, and regretting lots of decisions – and it feels so much because
you're not here to reassure/validate me and who I am. I suppose I should see
it as an opportunity to really forge that in myself without you – but it's hard.
And it's different. It's a different experience of validation. It's even different
to when Tim does – which he does all the time – but there's nothing like being
seen ... being seen by your mum. And God, I miss that.
I'm going to get the dress on Sunday. It will be weird to have completed
that whole process without you – one large aspect of getting married will be
complete.
I had a dream the other night that you were angry with me for neglecting
you. Do you feel I have been neglecting you? In the dream and when I woke
I really felt like I knew you were right – that I have been – but it's not that
I haven't been thinking about you, it's just more that I know I haven't been
'communing' with you – I haven't been letting you in.

There are times when I find it difficult to focus on my

161

grieving. At such times James feels a bit remote, a bit blurred in my mind. Like Annie, I feel that perhaps I am not communing with James; I need to be able to call him closer, to be able to throw him into sharp relief again. Perhaps it is nature's way of giving us a respite from grieving; for grief is hard, wearying work. We live it all the time, and some days or weeks are more difficult than others.

But this is where love comes in. It is a constant in our lives, whether it is maternal love, filial love, or the love for and from a friend. The love remains undimmed.

It is not always possible to work out why this remoteness happens, but perhaps the passage of time is significant here. The spells of less intense grief seem to have increased over the past few years, which I take to be a healthy sign, not a sign that I am forgetting, but that I am moving forward. Loving reminders of James are always welcome, whatever form they take.

There is an entirely specific type of love that you might encounter after loss that is described as 'compassionate love.' I am lucky indeed to have made some reciprocal compassionate, loving friendships since James died.

This love reaches out to you in your grief. It may come from people you hardly know, or it may come from those who have known you and your loved ones for a long time. It is a love that says, 'I am here, I am supporting you, I am in your shadow.' Compassionate love reflects the understanding, or attempt to understand, how the other person is feeling about their loss at any given time. It is an open, receptive form of love that has an equal value for both parties.

I believe it is also the love that can come to us from outside ourselves. It is godly, angelic, universal love.

Grief cuts through the superficiality of modern life. It is a raw emotion that is born of love, of all kinds.

Grief could be described as the necessary yang to the yin of love.

But ultimately, we realise that life is too short to be lived at the despondent, base level of grief. We find our priorities shift and change to put love at the top where it surely belongs; this is a natural response inbuilt in the human condition. No amount of debate by philosophers, learned theologians, or ordinary people like ourselves, can ever detract from the reality that love is key to meaning, structure and purpose in our lives.

I don't think that the introspection and self-examination which is often a feature of the newly bereaved is as closed as it might first appear.

When I think back to the early days, I can recall how desperate I was to find practical help and advice that would lead to my regaining some control and order to my chaotically disjointed thought processes. The challenge of concentrating and focusing on something other than grief can help surprisingly quickly.

There is not a single area in life that is not initially adversely affected by the enormity of grieving. Each of your senses, along with your appetite, heart, mind, body, soul and spirit, is jaded, knocked and battered to one degree or another.

Your relationships have to be redrawn overnight.

Your anxiety for the health and lifespan of everyone close to you is magnified out of all proportion.

You fear for your own health, wellbeing and sanity.

You may be numb or oversensitive; you may have periods of hysterical weeping or inappropriate laughter.

You are in a constant mode of adrenaline-rushing fight or flight.

You either cannot sleep or can't wake up.

Your world is reduced to the all-consuming personal awfulness of your loss.

All your terms of reference disappear.

Is it any wonder you need help to normalise all these effects? And how do you ratify the regret for what you cannot have in the future with the sorrow for what you have lost?

There are many tools in the grief toolbox.

Talking of how our lives have been shaped by the loss of our sons, Linda Sewell said to me,

"It is like BC and AD. I mean before the accident and after. There is simply no comparison."

I agree that there is a distinct delineation and we constantly have to work extremely hard to get through loss positively. The early months of grief are dominated by the *why* and *what if* questions. It is quite exhausting (but I think inevitable) to frequently replay what has happened over and over again, trying to make some sense of it, which of course is impossible at the start.

The ultimate emergence from the dark places of grief is a slow and hard-won process. It is a multi-faceted and highly individual progression upon which it is impossible to pin either timescale or rules. There are no rules when it comes to how you decide to approach your loss. There may be similarities in experiences, but no two grief paths will be entirely parallel.

Chapter 7
Golden Joinery

"They declared that they have found the earthy scent of petrichor, as if it was secretly drizzling in some deep corner of the city undetected by meteorologists. And when it rained on Monday, they smiled with pride and said: I told you so." [1]

Three times in a row, the word *petrichor* impinged on my consciousness. First, I heard it described on the radio. Then a visiting friend said the word after we had experienced a brief shower during a summer heatwave. Finally, I read a post on social media written by a friend of Shaun's, who was gently provoking people to wonder about the meaning of this unusual word.

Before then, I never knew there was a word for it: that distinctive, pleasant, earthy scent that is produced when rain falls on dry ground.

It smells the same wherever you are; a curious mix of stone, soil, bark, wet leaves and petals.

The word is petrichor.

It is an amalgam of the Greek for the words 'rock' and 'liquid' and it was coined in 1964 by two researchers. They pronounced that the smell derives from an oil exuded by plants which is absorbed by soil and rocks. When it rains, the oil is released back into the air and, along with by-products of certain bacteria the distinctive scent is produced.

If petrichor had a colour, I think it would be green: a damp-looking, subtle, mossy green.

Though the base notes of the scent of petrichor are always the same, yet it is variable. One day, after a rain shower, I noticed the petrichor had a different note; a sour, slightly acidic scent hinting at the onset of Autumn. Petunias and other annual flowers are past their best in late summer and beginning to set seed; that is the time when the plant scent element of the petrichor becomes quite strong.

I love that there is a scientific explanation for something as invisible but instantly recognisable as the aroma that is petrichor.

Trying to find a similarly scientific explanation for the way grief works, however, is a far more complex task. I live in the mourning light through living with the loss of James and other family members. But how exactly can I describe that light and the process by which I have reached it? There are so many components to it. They comprise the tools in the armoury of my grief toolbox.

Some are physical and visible: for example, writing and photography.

Some are represented by the connections I have with family and friends and the emotional and social support they provide.

Some are nebulous, like the practices of introspection and self-analysis.

Still others are rooted in my personal beliefs and my mode of spiritual connection through worship and prayer.

Everyday life events, such as walking the dog, shopping, socialising, preparing meals, are now done with a light-filled heart but that was not the case in darker times.

Each facet and element contribute to the light, in a similar way to that in which all the colours of the spectrum contribute to visible light.

I am by nature a pacifist, but grief makes me a warrior.

In simple terms, darkness is the enemy and light the friend, and fighting the darkness becomes an everyday part of life after loss. It feels like a battle; some skirmishes being more arduous than others. But I firmly believe that healing cannot happen, and the light cannot brighten, until the darkness has been lived in, examined and turned around, however painful that can be.

Allowing myself to feel the pain in darkness was the first step in comprehension that led me towards light. When the darkness seems endless, there is hope in the realisation that even after the darkest night, a new day will dawn. Is darkness the obverse side of light, or is light the obverse side of darkness? Either way they flip endlessly in their various shades.

Grief made me hyper-anxious and fearful. This was (and still is at times) one of the hardest elements to challenge, because anxiety feeds on itself.

It stacks up; at the beginning of the day, I had the fleeting thought, *"I wonder if Shaun's journey to work was OK this morning?"* by lunchtime this had become, *"I can't get hold of him, I hope everything is all right,"* and by tea time, *"He must have had an accident, I haven't heard from him all day!"* Five minutes later he walked through the door and wondered why I was in a mood!

The buzzword for this is 'catastrophising' and any griever is likely to recognise it. The relief when fears are not realised simply underlines how draining is the entire process.

Another catchword in counselling is 'ruminating' – not what cows do with their four stomachs, but the way in which you turn negative thoughts over and over in your head. This repetitive thinking is a hard pattern to break. The ideal way to get yourself off the worry train to shift focus. Over the years, I have practised mindful breathing when learning a variety of therapies, and if you can transfer the focus of your mind to the physical act of breathing, it can be very helpful. Another way to move yourself away from rumination is to engage in a diversionary activity, such as going for a walk, following a recipe or listening to some music, indeed anything that takes your mind off your intrusive thoughts.

Ask any bereaved parent and he or she will tell you that they quickly become experts at the art of diversion. You are constantly finding ways to deflect attention from the shocking facts of your loss.

C S Lewis said, *"No one ever told me that grief felt so like fear,"* [2] and he was right. It is a confidence sapper even for the strongest of grief warriors. There is also an ever-present fear of upsetting others with naked emotion; this is largely unfounded, I have discovered, when I have asked about this directly. Most people respond by saying that they are upset for and with you, not themselves, when they are supporting you in grief.

I have learned that grief is not static. It morphs into a resilience that you didn't know you had, and you know you are getting there when you can feel all right without feeling guilty that you feel all right!

Grief has a dark power that can be overcome with the strength of light and your reactions to it allow for a return to normal living, despite loss. If you can summon up the strength and courage to figuratively turn your back on grief's efforts to subsume you, you are on your way to recovery in the light.

There are facts about my loss that carry me through the

darkest of the darkness through which James's light will always shine.

I knew him from the time that I carried him in the rosy darkness of the womb.

I nurtured him for all the time he lived in the earth's light, and now I picture him in a different world of light. This gives me comfort.

Just as petrichor demonstrates a symbiotic partnership of rock and liquid, so the light, mourning or otherwise, needs the experience of the darkness to shine with true and solid strength.

Another word that came my way and which is a wonderful symbolism for all that is associated with grief is *Kintsugi*.

The Japanese word literally translates as 'golden joinery.' It is the art of repairing broken pottery with seams of gold. Metallic powder is added to adhesive and when the object is repaired, it becomes unique and more beautiful. Instead of the scars being hidden, they become a feature of the whole.

Kintsugi is not a new fad or trend. It dates from the fifteenth century when a Shogun broke one of his favourite tea bowls. He was unimpressed by shoddy mending and as a result he commissioned his workers to improve on what had been done. *Kintsugi* was the result.

Kintsugi can be a metaphor for life; it is a philosophy which embraces beauty and imperfections and is easy to take on board. The tenets are simple enough:

Though you are broken, you can be mended. People are like ceramics: strong, fragile and beautiful all at once. *Kintsugi* is evidence that you can heal your wounds. You can rebuild your life around the breaks and wear the scars with pride. They become part of you, and you become stronger and more resilient in the process.

Kintsugi is tangible, visible proof that your wounds eventually become scars that enhance you, rather than diminish. They may be tender to touch, but the wounds are no longer bleeding.

Kintsugi gives a gift of optimism characterised by a broken item that has been mended with something precious.

Kintsugi represents commendable, measurable strength and persistence in the face of adversity.

Kintsugi is beautifying rather than self-damaging.

All these years on since James died, I do not feel mended - don't think I will ever feel mended. But I feel that my golden scars have been created with a certain amount of combative pride. This pride comes from the ability to embrace my loss with resilience, and to seek out, find and live within the mourning light.

The mourning light is slowly and gradually dawned out of the darkness of grief and loss. For anyone who is newly bereaved this will be a hard concept to take on board. But you must trust in your own ability to heal, which takes patience and a proactive attitude. Throughout the process, you are gradually transformed by your hurts, just as the caterpillar is transformed into a butterfly.

My individual *Kintsugi* represents a fair amount (or unfair, depending on your perspective!) of grief and trauma; this is not said to engender pity but to underline how applying the principles embodied by *Kintsugi* can enrich, enhance and beautify your life.

Where do you find the gold for your own *Kintsugi* seams? You may find you need to adopt a new perspective that allows you to analyse the pain, trauma, difficulties and grief that you are living through. Then you use your knowledge to transform, as far as possible, negative into positive. Of course, not all scars are visible; for example, your psychological scars from the trauma of loss, but, you may be sharing your realisation that something has been taken from you that you can never get back, through the visual aid of *Kintsugi*.

When you apply *Kintsugi* principles to grief you are embracing a challenge. You meet it head on and you acknowledge the scars which are a testament to how you continue to live your life despite what has befallen you. You wear, bare and share these with fortitude and pride

You should try to mend what has been broken because the resultant creation is individual and more valuable for its flawed appearance.

In a similar way, the post bereavement mourning light is slightly opaque and diffuse compared to the light that went before. But it is powerful, and it undoubtedly reflects your new, normal way of living.

One of the best examples of *Kintsugi* I have seen is that of cancer survivors who are photographed with their visible scars, bravely sharing their transformation with the world. Their inner beauty shines through their physical imperfections. The scars cease to be what you see first.

Kintsugi is not simply about positivity. It is also to do with the choice of your response to whatever is broken. Loss through death breaks your relationship with your loved one as you knew it; and it is up to you how you reclaim it. The beauty of *Kintsugi* is that the way you do that is entirely your choice.

When I broke two small ceramic bowls recently, in the act of carelessly pulling a plate from the cupboard, I wish I had known about *Kintsugi*. Instead of regretfully throwing the pieces into the bin, I would have carefully repaired the bowls and displayed them proudly with their golden scars. It is an important lesson learned.

Much has woven itself into my own personal representation

of *Kintsugi*.

Over the years since James died, a variety of individuals have become known to me. Connections have been made that I could never have imagined.

Doors have opened to me that would otherwise have remained closed.

Perhaps most importantly, friendships have developed which would not otherwise have existed.

My personal growth and development, knowledge of my own trinity of mind, body and spirit and how they work together - and against each other - in the grief process – all of these evolved from the truly awful loss that I experienced.

Nothing can ever fully mend or compensate for the absence of James but the ongoing efforts – not just mine, but of everyone who knew him, and many others who did not, contribute to the prevention of future loss. My support comes from many and varied sources, each having their own place in uplifting me in my heartbreak.

There is no denying that the death of a loved one is shattering in every sense of the word. But the importance of piecing life together again is paramount. Something destructive can, and does, lead to something productive if you can use the building blocks garnered from all different directions. I refer often to the grief toolbox. *Kintsugi* is the latest in a long line of aids for me. I was reminded last summer of how it feels to heal from loss when I was struggling to climb a steep slope of sand dunes. For every step up that I took, the sand shifted beneath my feet and I slid back. It was a long, hard, hot climb. How like the grief path, which represents an exaggeration of 'two steps forward, one step back.'

If you are someone who is working through grief's non-linear, supremely challenging stages you should feel a huge amount of pride at what you achieve and how you present to the world.

I say to anyone who is grieving,

"Look to your own wounds. Think about your personal healing process. Find the beauty in your scars and wear them with pride."

One of my deepest scars came in 2001 when I lost my mum. There was the woman I was before, and the woman I was afterwards. That grief was, at the time, my hardest experience ever. I learned much about the sheer weight of grief, and how heavy a burden it is to carry. I learned to shoulder it through focusing on all the happy times we had shared and trying to emulate her particular brand of positive living. Mum was a happy person who always saw the best in others and she never wasted energy on the negative aspects of life.

My ex-husband Ken died in November 2002, and this loss

brought its own particular difficulties, especially for my teenage children who had to learn to cope with losing a parent at such a young age. Our square of four became a triangle of three in 2002 and it was very tough on all of us. The only positive I could take is that when a spouse dies, there is the consolation that you knew a life before they came into yours, and it is possible to envisage a future without them. I had already learned to look forward following our separation. This helped to a degree, but it was a challenging period.

Then in November 2017, cancer took my brother Peter, and this grief remains raw and unfinished in terms of how I work through it. Whether or not you are close, to lose a sibling is to lose a person with whom you expected to grow old. My sense of loss at Peter's passing is profound. Our relationship ebbed and flowed over the years. Thankfully it was harmonious in recent times. I know I will miss seeing his handwriting on the envelopes at birthday and Christmas times – whatever else was going on, he always sent cards. I have lost the person who remembered things about our parents that I cannot. Our family stories suddenly have to be told from a single perspective. A sibling represents a person's past, present, and future and this makes it a particularly difficult grief to assimilate, whatever your age at the time.

Regardless of which kind of grief you survive, you won't and can't be the same person you were before loss, but that shouldn't necessarily be seen as a bad thing.

You have to want to live despite your losses, and you have to want to live well. You are here and they are not, and it is important for you to live the best possible life you can, enjoy the fullest days imaginable, to make up for all those lost days that your loved ones are missing. Yes, you will exist in a kind of grey fog for a while, but natural resilience and optimism are just around the corner if you can but find them.

Grief lays you bare; it is isolating, and it hurts in a way that no other life experience hurts. Sometimes I think that the grief I experienced in losing my parents and my ex-husband were some kind of God-sent preparation for the worst grief of all when we lost James in 2005. It is only in recent times that I have drawn strength from believing in God's helping hand that brings me through all my difficult times.

There have been many occasions over the years when someone, learning that I have lost a child, has said, *"Oh, I can't imagine what it must be like to lose a child."* My response, if I were brave enough to voice it, would be to say: *"No you can't, and I wouldn't want you to have to experience it.*

But know that if you are unfortunate enough to do so, you can live through

179

it and you will emerge from the darkness of grief and loss into the mourning light over time." As it is with all grief and all loss.

In writing, I find consolation in the stock of stories, images and allegories that I get from faith. They're accessible to everyone and that underlines that you are not alone. Everything that I experience has been experienced before, down the ages. Grief is nothing new.

In the early days of loss, I would have struggled to empathise much with anyone mourning the loss of a pet, but I understand more now about the layers of love, loss and grief that life experience can throw our way. I am more generous-hearted these days, now that my own grief is a gentler thing.

Grief is forever, but it morphs itself endlessly into different shapes and forms. Sometimes they stand before you like sentries preventing you getting past; at other times they walk quietly in your shadow.

Grief and love are intertwined in a curious way. I am reminded of what happens when you mix oil and vinegar. The two separate ingredients agitate together until they form a smooth emulsion. The balm of love and grief combined allows you to think of those you have lost with affection, and with a smile first before tears.

Every year on the anniversary of James's passing, I receive a thoughtful letter from Pat, a fellow medical secretary with whom I worked at St Peter's Hospital, Chertsey, back in the late 1980s. We have kept in touch over the years, along with others from that period, the closest being my dear friend Pauline who continues to be a great support to me and is someone else who enjoys sharing her memories of James. Pat and Pauline both knew Stella and James from their very young days, and I know they hold loving memories of them. I knew that Pat would be willing to share her feelings around James apropos love and grief. She says:

'For me, love most definitely does endure after death, but how to write about it is a different matter.

Does everyone feel the same when they have lost someone dear to them?

Is it the same if it's not a loved one, but perhaps just a close friend?

I really didn't know.

It's not the kind of thing you bring up over coffee, is it? I started to think about some of those people who have walked along life's road with me, some for a short time, others much longer. They have one thing in common; sadly they are no longer with me.

I first met Andrea's children Stella and James, when they were quite small. James wasn't yet at school. Sometimes Andrea would bring them in to work with her. I'm not sure why but James was to become a complete delight to me. With his blonde hair, big eyes and cheeky grin, he won my heart.

We had great fun when his mum would send him along to my office to 'see if Pat has something you can do!' His favourite task was to use the shredder (it got a lot of use) and he diligently set to, although I sometimes only just managed to rescue something important in the nick of time!

When James started losing his baby teeth, I started writing notes for him in silver ink, "from the tooth fairy." He loved the notes. I don't know when James finally realised that there wasn't really a fairy writing to him, but I missed writing from her! As he grew up, Andrea left for a new job elsewhere, and I didn't see James again, but I always thought about him.

When I heard of his death in 2005, my first thoughts were of course for his family. How on earth do you live with such a tragedy? I couldn't begin to imagine their pain. I grieved for the future James wouldn't have.

James's funeral was full of colour; sadness obviously, but also lots of good memories shared by many. For me, James will always be the same golden-haired little boy I shared laughs with. I think of him often, just odd things bring his face to mind and make me smile.

Although it wasn't love I felt for him in the way we usually think of love, something … fondness perhaps, keeps him in my heart.

I have lost both my parents now, and I feel their love with me every day. It warms and comforts me, but is this how other people feel about the loss of a loved one or dear friend?

I still didn't really know.

I watch the November Remembrance Service at the Cenotaph every year because I was brought up to treat this as a special day, but in 2016, watching the service, it suddenly hit me; watching the veterans and the many different groups marching past the Cenotaph paying homage to lost comrades, fathers, sons, brothers, and now, mothers, daughters and sisters, listening to them speak so lovingly about those they loved and lost, I saw that they all shared a very important thing; one feeling common to them all – a strong love that has endured, for some, for 70 years after death. For some it is more recent, but this love has kept the ones they love bright and alive in their memories, bringing them some form of comfort.

Just before Christmas 2016, two of my friends lost their husbands within a day of each other. I no longer live in the UK; my husband John and I have settled in France. I was unable to be with my friends; what comfort I could offer had to be over the 'phone. I could feel their grief, and I shared it because both couples were friends of ours. We also feel a great loss.

These two ladies are starting to move through the grieving process, and it is of course very hard for them. As anyone who has lost someone dear to them knows, it takes time.

One of them was recently taken out for the evening, and I asked her,

"Did you manage to enjoy at least a little of the show you were taken to see?"

She replied,

"Yes, I did, but I shed tears when I thought about how much my husband would have enjoyed it."

Both these women feel the presence of their husbands around them and it brings them some peace, so perhaps this is love continuing. I like to think it is.

So … do we need more proof that love does not fade or die just because those we love have died? I don't think so. Our love for those we miss, and theirs for us will continue to comfort us and be with us always. We just need to open our hearts to it."

Holding on to the memories of those whom we love and have lost is not in itself a difficult thing to do when you are past the first agonies of grieving. My dear friend Sylvi died in September 2016 and I think of her often, and especially around the anniversary of her passing.

Sylvi was a woman of immense warmth and kindness, and at the time we met in the 1980s it felt as though she scooped me up and bore me off to places I had never been before.

This was literally true, as she introduced me to the RHS gardens at Wisley and thus began my lifelong affinity with plants and flowers.

Sylvi was a teacher by profession and a teacher by nature and I learned much under her tutelage, from tending hydrangeas to how to bake chocolate cake in the microwave.

She moved from Surrey to Somerset when the children were still young, but the distance did not detract from our friendship.

We met several times a year, usually child free, for lovely days of talks and window-shopping in Salisbury which was about equidistant from our homes. We were very much in tune. More than once we turned up with the same recently read book to lend each other.

Sylvi remarried and ultimately, she and her husband Tim

settled in France. They lived near Confolens and then moved to the Languedoc region. Throughout the years, we kept in touch through letters, telephone calls and visits. Our letters chronicled the ups and downs of our lives and despite the advent of the internet, we continued to write to each other through the medium of pen and paper. Sylvi had a way of drawing pictures with words and her letters were invariably entertaining. She always signed off, *"Fondest Love, Sylvi"* and I knew she meant it.

Stella and James had happy memories of visits to Sylvi in the school holidays. Perhaps my memories are rose-tinted, but the sun always seemed to shine and the children happily camped out in the garden.

We kept up with the progression of them all through childhood: Stella, James, Lucy, Hollie, Mel and David.

Sadly, Sylvi was diagnosed with cancer in 2013 but she lived her remaining time with amazing fortitude, defying successive prognoses, ultimately succumbing in September 2016.

The love that exists between two female friends is a gentle, forgiving and empathic kind of love. We are lucky if we experience it with more than a handful of friends throughout our life.

Ours was just such a close and loving friendship.

We never had a cross word in all our years of knowing

each other. We could tell each other anything, which is a measure of true friendship. Whenever we met, even after long gaps it was as though we had seen each other the day before – another measure of true friendship.

We were not judgemental of each other's actions; we were mutually supportive and provided a shoulder to cry on or a good laugh as the occasion demanded.

At the time of James's funeral service in 2005, Sylvi sat in the small chapel in St Germain de Confolens to be with us in spirit; the action of a very loving friend.

Afterwards, she sent me a note and photographs she had taken in the chapel at the time, both keepsakes to treasure.

I miss Sylvi for being one of my first go-to people with any news, good or bad, and as such she is irreplaceable.

In Spring 2017 Shaun and I joined a gathering to commemorate Sylvi; an informal ceremony that saw her daughters, sisters and husband committing her ashes to the ocean. Sylvi's funeral had taken place in France but her wishes were that she would be brought to Lyme Regis in Dorset.

This was one of her favourite places, significantly for Christmas morning picnics with the family, regardless of the weather.

We drew together from near and far; family, colleagues and friends each holding our own memories of Sylvi as mother, grandmother, sister, wife, friend. We walked and talked together as we navigated the very uneven pebbly beach, gravitating to a quiet spot that Tim chose as the place where our informal committal would attract least notice.

The sun shone brightly, glittering off the sea.

We gathered round the family and stood at a respectful distance as Lucy read some well-constructed words and we were handed yellow roses to throw into the water.

Lucy, Hollie, Tim and Sylvi's sisters Hazel and Annie each took a turn to commit some ashes to the sea.

This started off with sombre decorum, but before long Lucy and Hollie kicked off their shoes and braved the undoubtedly cold water to lovingly send off their mum.

There was something incredibly, powerfully touching about watching these two strong, beautiful young women standing in the shallows and little by little, saying such a personal and utterly connected goodbye to the mum they so dearly loved. The ebb and flow of the tide would carry her away gently and silently.

Afterwards, Hollie wrote (and I share with her permission),

"Holding my mother in ashes in my own palm was a strange but unique feeling; she had held my hand, held me and held my heart more times than is possible to count and today was our turn to hold her and let her go.

My lesson from today for myself and others is enjoy every minute with your loved ones, make the effort, say how you feel and don't be afraid to say or show it."

Water gives life, it sustains life, and in this case, it absorbed the last remnants of a life in a spiritually uplifting, natural way. It was so good to see the repression usually associated with modern grief being cast aside in favour of such a memorable and simple committal to nature.

Throwing our roses into the sea allowed us to share in the precious and unique event and send our messages to Sylvi's waterborne spirit.

I am glad to have ongoing close contact with Sylvi's daughter Lucy and her husband Dan, and their daughter Amelie, as well as Hollie in Wales and Mel in Somerset.

Through all this contact, the stories of our friendship continue to be told and memories are shared.

Lucy and Dan's wedding in early 2016 was the last occasion I was able to spend time with Sylvi and I remember her saying the following morning that, throughout the wedding day, *"The room was filled with so much love."*

We knew we were saying our last goodbye though neither of us acknowledged it.

Sylvi's ashes being committed to the ocean in 2017 was an entirely fitting way for my lovely friend to be remembered.

I miss you, Sylvi. Fondest Love.

Chapter 8

Transformational Gifts

"Maybe some people just aren't meant to be in our lives forever. Maybe some people are just passing through. It's like some people just come through our lives to bring us something: a gift, a blessing, a lesson we need to learn. And that's why they're here. You'll have that gift forever." Danielle Steele[1]

The concept that grief and loss can give us anything other than pain and heartache, indeed that they may provide something of a positive nature, is an entirely untenable idea in the early stages of bereavement. But as we progress along our individual grieving process in the somewhat hesitant and turbulent manner associated with living with loss, we may find ourselves surprised.

Very soon after James passed, I began to write out my feelings as a way of alleviating my pain. Writing is solace for me and I have always expressed myself in written form, usually keeping journals and diaries for my eyes only. I recognise myself as a recorder of events; if I am not photographing it, I am writing it down! I began to share my writing on grief support forums and the first time someone kindly commented, saying,

"Your words have really helped me; you have expressed exactly what I am feeling."

I felt tremendously uplifted.

All the words we have at our disposal, whether heard or spoken, read or written, have the potential to bring the gift of comfort in loss and grief.

I really don't write for plaudits and praise, but there is great satisfaction in knowing that what comes relatively easily to me can help others in similar situations.

This was an unexpected outcome from loss and the first of its identifiable gifts.

The catharsis of the act itself, the practice of it, and keeping James's memory alive through writing about him benefit me, too.

Alongside writing, I have on occasion been asked to speak about grief and I've given a number of presentations, both formal and informal. Public speaking was never within my remit before. But it brings a very important message, which is that grief has given me a new voice, a positive voice that shares the state of mind around the rollercoaster ride of sorrow in a way that uplifts and helps those who are travelling a similar route.

This second gift takes its form as a growing confidence which arises directly from my experiences and is therefore very personal. I retain control of what I share about my family and in particular, my son. I make conscious decisions about how much, or how little, I am prepared to divulge of the very essence of our family. Public grieving carries with it vulnerability, the potential to be inspected and/or judged in ways that are too intrusive. There are numerous examples of this for people in the public eye ... a good example being our Royal Family, whom I suspect are sometimes utterly fed up with the minutest details of their lives being made public.

The grief of my family and James's story may be considered small fry in the face of this, though the Queen herself has not lost a son. Yet how is it any different if you are laying bare your emotions and family life? It is something worth considering should you be deciding whether to go public with your own story.

The third gift from loss with which I identify is that of resilience. I write more of this in Chapter 10, but I am touching on it here because it is such an important attribute on which to reflect when considering how we carry on living meaningfully after loss.

When we were on holiday in 2015, I made a less than sensible decision. We arrived at a most beautiful location, the port of Kotor in Montenegro. Above the city, itself bounded by ancient walls, is a zigzag, vertiginous cliff path up the side of the mountain which rises from the fjord on which Kotor is located. Despite my mobility being significantly compromised by my arthritic hip, I was determined that I would ascend the path, reaching at the very least halfway up, in my quest for photographs.

We set off. It was hot, steep and dusty. The path was heavy going, made treacherous with loose shale. But I was constantly seeking the best photo opportunities as we ascended, and I concentrated on reaching the goal. We finally made it; hot and sweaty but with the sense of achievement that comes only from working through something difficult; and in this case painful.

This example illustrates that there is no recompense in just sitting brooding and reflecting on grief, loss and sadness. We need to hold onto the faith in our ability to metaphorically climb mountains as they loom up ahead of us.

The result is the gift of knowing that we have the resilience that says we are managing, we are coping, and we are working our way forward, however long and difficult the climb.

I didn't do myself any favours in Kotor as this unwise expedition turned out to be the defining factor in my decision to seek a hip replacement on our return home. Fortunately, this went very well, and I was able to call upon my reserves of resilience once again to give me the determination to get mobile. The gift inherent in that trek up the mountain was to give me a clearer vision about what I needed to do for the sake of my future.

If we open our minds and hearts with faith in our own strength we can draw upon many forms of support, both seen and unseen, which then nurture and bolster our determination to carry on progressing in personal grief terms. It is only by moving forward that we are able to look back down the weeks, months and years and chart our advancement.

The signposts and helpers along the way point us towards what eventually become tangible positives; such are our gifts from loss.

The gift of being a parent in the first place is the greatest gift of all. When James died in 2005, I asked myself, *"Am I still mother to a son and a daughter?"* The answer is, of course I am! I did not stop being my mother's daughter when my mum died, so I should not consider myself any less of a mother because my son died.

I am still myself.

First and foremost, I am me, and I was granted the gift of motherhood twice.

Nothing detracts from that, even though one of my children is no longer here.

Becoming a mother to two beautiful children remains my biggest ever life achievement.

Memories are perhaps the greatest gift we have to sustain us in loss of our loved ones. I hold close to me the memories that are engendered in particular by photographs of James. There are many; from his babyhood until shortly before his death. As I have said before, we are great recorders in our family – photography rather than video being our medium of choice.

But there is a tiny video clip of James which I have on my PC and I have watched it over and over again, when I want to re-establish in my memory the way he stood, his stance, his expression, and the way he moved. He was in a crowd and I can pick out his chuckle. I would know his voice anywhere and forever. In fact, hearing him is one of the aspects I miss the most and now I wish I had far more film of him.

A while ago, I had my late father's collection of cine films covering the early 1960s collated into a DVD. These short silent clips are extremely emotive to watch. There was my mum, smiling and youthful, and there were my brother and I, awkwardly shuffling from one foot to the other and waving and grinning to Dad on cue.

There was a wonderful clip shot in Dad's Vauxhall Velox car showing a virtually deserted M1 motorway and the speedometer inching towards 100mph – dad was always a bit of a speed freak and I well remember our day trip dashes to his friends in Staffordshire.

Seeing this film made me long for more footage of James, but alas it does not exist. This could be a timely reminder to anyone reading this to make a short film of your family and friends – so easy to do these days with mobile phones and keep it for posterity on a PC somewhere or have it put onto DVD.

I think it is fair to say that bereaved parents develop an extreme sensitivity to emotion. Regardless of how we lost our child, our compassion to those who are newly bereaved becomes more evident as time goes on and we feel more able to reach out to others than introspectively processing our loss. Somehow, we literally feel things differently because of our loss and I think this applies to positive as well as negative emotions.

Our responses may be dampened down in the early shock of grief, but when they regrow, they generate slightly differently. I know that my radar for others' moods is greater than it used to be. I can speak for many other bereaved parents when I say I know their awareness of emotional distress is far greater, as is my own. We have learned, perhaps, the right things to say, through our own difficult lessons.

People worry that they will offend or distress the bereaved by mentioning the person who has died, but it is quite the opposite. I cannot envisage a time that I will not wish to remember James, to talk about him, to share reminiscences and anecdotes.

He was no saint - he could be immensely irritating, and I often laugh at those memories too. As a child he was a terrible screecher.

He was often in trouble at school, he was on report more than he was off it and I was frequently called in to see the Head Teacher, always with great trepidation as to what he had done.

One of his worst misdemeanours was to persuade one of his classmates to have his ear pierced. This event took place on a school trip! It may be funny in retrospect although it certainly was not at the time. In particular because the child in question was underage, the school could have been held responsible. In the event, the offending earring was removed, the child's ear closed up and James was forgiven. Just imagine if it had been a tattoo!

I find that I like to eke out sharing my memories of James, so that I do not run out of them. They are by their nature limited. But the contributions of others, and things that might jog my own memory, are indeed like gold to me.

Something dreadful happens to your confidence when you lose your child. It disappears like bathwater down the plughole, draining away and leaving you feeling like a hollow shell.

I well remember that time in early loss, being quite incapable of making the simplest mundane decisions, yet I had to arrange my son's funeral, a traumatic task that defies comment.

But the good news is that you will in time become a reasonably similar version of who you were before.

I remember reading an article by American grief counsellor Mitch Carmody in which he spoke of the bereaved parent living life a heartbeat behind everyone else; it is as though our timeframe has slipped slightly. Mitch is right, but I have found that sensation does lessen over time.

I believe that being at the very brink of endurance imbues the bereaved with a different kind of strength.

We have all read of superhuman feats - *"man lifts car to save passenger"* - and looked in awe at the Iron Man challenges undertaken by athletes that push them to the absolute limit.

It strikes me as very interesting that so many bereaved parents go on to achieve things in their lives which require strength, and above all, confidence.

I know several bereaved parents who now express themselves as writers and artists.

I know those who have challenged authority and won, those who campaign with organisations overseas and make a difference.

I know those whose fundraising efforts in memory of their children are tireless.

I know some who have moved to a different area to successfully make a different life.

Others conquer phobias and say, *"Now I feel more normal"* - whatever that means! These positive changes are in themselves unexpected gifts coming out of loss.

Nothing that life throws at you afterwards is ever going to be as bad as what you have faced and survived; and when you conquer things, large or small, that make you anxious or nervous, you are drawing on many new strengths and gifts. For some their strength may come from faith or spiritual belief. For myself, it tends to be a little bit of everything (after all, everyone knows I have a toolbox for my grief) and undoubtedly the love and support around me, both seen and unseen, ensures that I hold my head high and walk through life with greater force and purpose these days.

This new strength and confidence are important gifts we should harness and embrace to take us forward in our lives without our beloved children

I have also discovered those seemingly random occurrences that bring comfort in unexpected ways.

In 2014 we were on holiday in Phuket, Thailand, and took a boat trip that involved time spent on the main boat, and also being taken around caves and lagoons by canoe, with a Thai crew member acting as our guide, who paddled the canoe for our safety.

There were seven couples on the boat, we waited in turn to be allocated to a crew member and step off onto our canoe. Thai names tend to be unpronounceable to Europeans, so the crew members adopt short names that are easily remembered. Somehow, I was not really that surprised that our crewman introduced himself as James.

He was about as dissimilar from our James as you could possibly be, being a dark-eyed, thickset, stolid looking chap. But he was kind, courteous and funny as we have found most Thais to be. He chatted to us and laughed with us as we wobbled our way off the boat into his small canoe, figuratively putting our lives into a stranger's hands. He gently handed me into the canoe and made sure I was comfortably seated in the small space. How strange it felt to be saying, *"Thank you, James,"* after all this time. Also sharing little jokes and saying, *"You are funny, James, you do make me laugh,"* and so on.

There was an acute poignancy in those few hours in having my son's name so frequently upon my lips.

Strangely, later on in the day I overheard a conversation on the boat between two of the passengers. It transpired that one of them, a lady from India, had also lost a son.

What are the odds, I wonder, of there being two bereaved mothers from either side of the world, in such a small group, on the same boat trip, on the same day? I did not get the opportunity to speak to the woman before we went our separate ways, but I found it an odd coincidence. It is indeed true that everyone has a story, and sometimes we are destined to share these, sometimes not. Circumstances did not dictate that our paths crossed directly, but I still find it unusual that we were in the same place at the same time. Perhaps it was a missed opportunity. But I have learned as I have gone along in this regard. Sometimes it is good to share, and at other times someone else's story is key, not mine. My story didn't matter to that individual on that occasion, and there was no need for me to share it then.

Another seemingly random sign came our way which was poignant, but it made us laugh. We were invited by the RNLI to their headquarters in Poole, Dorset, when I first became involved in the Respect the Water campaign in 2014.

We attended a meeting at the campaign office and were then free to enjoy the hospitality at the RNLI College which is also a hotel (and highly recommended as a base for a weekend away).

We were booked onto a complimentary guided tour of

the college which is offered to visitors. This was very interesting and gave us extra insight into the work done by the RNLI.

We moved as a group into the area above the training pool where we were told about the exercises which are carried out there. My eye was immediately drawn to a table on the far side of the room. On the table, incongruously, sat a vacuum cleaner. Nothing odd about that, you may say … but the vacuum cleaner was of a make which produces machines with names (most commonly Henry). This bright yellow model sported, in large letters, the name JAMES. *"Psst ..."* I nudged Shaun. *"Look at that!"*

He followed my gaze and neither of us could help laughing at this unusual spiritual sign. Later we toasted James as we sat in the evening sunshine overlooking the harbour and marvelled at the mystery of it all.

In management circles, there are a number of different types of leadership. There are two I am focussing on here which I think correlate very well with how you respond to grief and loss.

Transactional leadership is described as the role of supervision, organisation and group performance. Transactional leaders are concerned about day to day progress towards goals.

Transformational leadership, on the other hand, is a

form of leadership whereby followers are motivated and engaged, rather than just going through the motions. It seems to me that transactional leadership is reactive, but transformational leadership is proactive and seeks out positive change.

If these tenets are applied to the grieving process it is easy to see how they would affect you differently. Transactional grief would see you coping on a day to day level, but perhaps not being sufficiently motivated to move forward and process your loss positively. Transactional grief might be said to see you stuck on a treadmill where the pace is static. You are literally existing, rather than living, and joy and optimism are in short supply. Finding the trigger to move you forward into a different pace of grieving may take a long time to come, if at all.

If you are grieving in a transactional way, you might be thinking something like this:

'I have often questioned 'whether I was a 'good enough' mother. Throughout my children's upbringing it was a question I asked myself fairly regularly. But it is no good now, playing the game of 'what if? because I know in my heart, and I have the faith to believe, that what happened to James was *meant* to happen. There is nothing that I or anyone else could have done to prevent the accident of his death when it occurred. Guilt is one of the worst aspects of bereavement. As a mother, I feel guilty that I could not protect my son from the ultimate harm that befell him. Did I teach him well enough? Should I, could I, have done more? Why us … why him … why me?'

I had to stop asking myself these questions because they prevented me from moving forward in the grieving process.

Yet I believe they were inevitable, valid questions to ask at the time, though they must remain unanswered. I did the best job I could in bringing up my children and that is the most that any parent can ever do.

We put our children's happiness and well-being ahead of our own. We do this not in any expectation of reward, but in love and devotion to those wonderful beings we have nurtured and produced. We may feel we are doing it all wrong – after all, there is no rule book – but almost invariably we are doing it right – or the best right that we can manage. This is one of the reasons we feel so devastated by the loss of a child – simply because we feel we should have been able to protect him or her and stop it from happening. In transactional grief, you never get past this cycle of loss, grief, guilt, pain and sadness. It is all too easy to get bound up in the negativity of regret for the past instead of looking for positivity for the future.

Transformational grief would see you grieving proactively

and measuring your progress over time in leaps, bounds and steps. Hindsight is a wonderful thing in transformational grief, because you can look back and measure how far you have travelled.

I miss my mother's presence though it is many years since she died; I miss my son's presence in an entirely different way.

Mum lived a relatively long life, and her death was part of the cycle of life and death that we recognise as the norm. But James's death came almost before his life had properly begun and this carries particular regret and poignancy, for all the years of life that he should have had before him but will not now experience.

Living each day with these absences makes me value even more the gift of the memories of the presence of my mother and my son.

Sophocles said,[2] *"Children are the anchors that hold a mother to life."* I have lost one of my anchors but the importance of being a mother remains key to my living my life with as much joy and positivity as I can manage.

Some people are able to demonstrate the transformational nature of grief in very tangible fashion.

Author Annie Broadbent, whose contribution appears in Chapter 6, very kindly invited me to attend the launch of her book, *We Need to Talk about Grief*, (now republished as

Speaking of Death) which she wrote following the loss of her mother to cancer.

Annie was just twenty-five when her mum Caroline died. Annie and I were put in (electronic) touch, through her agent who 'thought we might get on' and so it proved. I recognise in Annie a kindred writing spirit. Though we approach grief from entirely diverse viewpoints due to the differing nature of our losses, we share the desire to strip away the inhibitions and taboos surrounding the business of death and dying. Despite our age difference we write in a similar way, sharing deep emotions; and ultimately offering the message of positivity and hope for the future. Grief is grief, whether you have lost a parent or a child, and the commonality of this is reflected in the writing of us both.

Annie's speech at the launch of her book was moving and expressive and I know that she felt the same sense of elation that I did when my first book was published, albeit we both know that the emotion is invariably tempered with regret for the reason for writing in the first place..

How refreshing it was during that event, to be in the company of people who did not flinch, look uncomfortable or try to change the subject when I said the words, *"My son James died."*

As one lady said to me, *"There will be a lot of talk of death and dying tonight; there are plenty of experts here,"* but the atmosphere was not dark and dismal, rather there was much compassion, empathy, sharing and laughter. Other cultures and people with alternative views around the world can talk of death and dying without feeling guilty, and with a more open attitude. Perhaps we in the west need to learn some of the lessons brought to us through globalisation that can help us to better confront these issues.

I feel privileged to have met and mingled briefly with these lovely people who shared a positive and transformational approach to loss.

Annie herself is a vibrant, warm girl and her mother was obviously held in high regard. I formed an impression of an equally warm and charming woman with more than a hint of mischief about her. She sounded like the best kind of mum, the kind that I was also fortunate enough to have.

Annie says of her book, *"This is a book filled with personal experiences which are designed to open up a conversation,"* which fits beautifully with her title and I agree wholeheartedly with the need for a more open attitude towards the topics surrounding bereavement. I am certain that Annie's book will help many people living with the loss of their loved ones.

I am grateful to Annie, for inviting me to share in such a special moment in her life and for further contributing some of her later thoughts in the form of a letter to her mum, in Chapter 6.

Visual gifts are also important in processing loss. On occasion I have been to see and photograph the tropical butterfly display in the glasshouse at the gardens owned by the Royal Horticultural Society (RHS Wisley). This annual event is very popular. Getting good images of the butterflies is something of a challenge. Firstly, the humidity in the glasshouse fogs the lens; though it will eventually clear. Butterflies are notoriously camera shy and will perch on a leaf just ever so slightly beyond your camera's point of focus... but despite this, I have usually been pleased with my shots.

But it was a butterfly I saw outside that really caught my attention last time I was there with my camera. It is most unusual to see one of our native butterflies in February, but it was a sunny day and I imagine this Red Admiral may have been fooled by thoughts of a false spring.

I realised as I photographed it that images own a special place as a representation of grief. Photographers learn about depth of field – particularly in close up shots. Depth of field is the area of sharpness (from near to far) within a photograph. With modern cameras and a little knowledge of their settings, it is possible to focus on the foreground and put the background out of focus, and vice versa. Selective focus sees a chosen part of the image thrown into sharp relief against a blurred background. In theory, a lens is able to focus on only one object at a time and I wonder if grieving is so very different. The early days of my loss transposed to a photograph would have had the focal point of James standing out vividly and sharply against a dull and monochrome background.

I well remember that every single waking moment included something of James in it. Nothing else around me held any significance. I was not interested in what was going on around me. Local, national and international happenings blurred into the background – and that was entirely right for that period of mourning.

An ideal place to be in grieving is akin to the photograph that is a 'storytelling exposure' – an image that shows broad depth of field. The main emphasis of your image and the surrounding background are all in equal focus, balanced and level. No one thing stands out more than another.

I took one of my favourite images of James when on a visit to him at Brighton University in 2004. This is definitely a storytelling exposure; there is a little boy in the background who reminds me of James when he was young, and James looks so happy and relaxed. It was a lovely day that I hold close in my heart.

Today, at moments when my grief for my son is a bit

blurry, I sense a need to take the time to look at some photos, or recall in my mind some of our time together, to bring everything back into focus and relocate it to the 'right' place for my day to day life.

I recently heard my friend Linda Sewell describe it as 'being given gold' when a friend of her son Tom sent her some images that she had not seen before.

I understand entirely what she means.

I treasure all the images of James that I have, and because like me, he was a keen photographer, he also amassed boxes of them; some of which I have yet to scan in to keep on electronic file. Most of his photos were taken with a film camera, so they are hard copy rather than on the computer. Digital photography, online photo sharing and storage was in its infancy when he died. I love looking at the photos but have to be in the right mood so that they do not leave residual distress. Naturally, I have a deep sense of loss that there cannot be any new images and that is a facet of my grief that is hard to assimilate at times. The safety and security that we experience at home, in our own particular comfort zone, is a gift of another kind. Being cast adrift without our usual visual compass can take you back to the early stages of grief in an instant.

On the road driving back from Cornwall a while ago, this was very clearly illustrated to me.

Soon after I set off, I drove into thick fog on the A30 – an open, windswept road that can appear bleak in all but the best of weathers.

Immediately, all terms of reference for everything around me disappeared; my world was reduced to the cocooning surround of the car and my focus was limited entirely to the road ahead. It was scary. Vehicles travelling in the opposite direction loomed eerily out of the half-light and my gaze became fixed on the red lights of the vehicles ahead, which were the only beacons I could follow. Every so often, there were little pockets of clarity in the gloom, which threw objects into sharp relief against the shrouding mist … here was a farmhouse set back from the road, there was a sign for riding stables. But these side issues failed to make any impact on me, such was my need for concentration on the road ahead.

I could not help but draw a parallel with how life is changed by loss; in a moment one is thrown into an abyss of confusion, despair and despondency that feels like a claustrophobic corridor. We cannot turn back but must face forward and fix our gaze upon what lies ahead. What has gone before impedes progress, but we learn that we must move forward. The issues around us barely impinge on our consciousness; such is our single-minded attention to the overwhelming demands of grief.

As I simultaneously drove along, listened to the radio, concentrated on the cars in front of me, and thought myriad thoughts, I considered how amazingly adept we are at being able to divaricate our minds when we have to. Hence, even in the early stages of loss and grieving, we are able to continue to function on an ordinary level *somehow* – sleeping, waking, shopping, cooking, cleaning, driving, walking, working …. All the time processing and working through what has happened to us. We truly can, and do, multi-task.

I have driven along the same stretch of the A30 many times and it is a familiar route to me; yet when the fog descended, I felt as though I had no idea where I had come from, or where I was going. I felt invisible and as though my confidence had been pulled like a rug from beneath my feet. I was frightened and had to quell a growing sense of panic, reassuring myself that it would not be long until I came out the other side of the fog.

I longed for the familiarity of home and began to count the hours and minutes until I reached my safe haven. I visualised arriving and being welcomed home by Shaun, making a cup of tea and unpacking my case – all the normal, ordinary things that we do when we get home after a spell away.

However, in early grief, even the place we call home

can lose its status as our secure and safe place to be. I remember feeling this very strongly because home is where I learned of James's death, and home suddenly became an alien environment filled with memories of him, rather than his presence.

Home should not be where bad things happen. Though I should qualify this by saying that for those who choose to be at home for a 'managed' passing, the outcome is entirely different. This provides for people to have comforting memories that their loved one has spent their last days on earth, at home, in familiar surroundings.

But for us, it was very difficult to learn to dissociate home from what had happened, and it took a long time. There was a kind of traumatic residue that never really disappeared for the remainder of the time we lived in the property. Little wisps of it remained like mist that failed to dissipate.

I write often of the grief journey being one of moving from darkness back into light; but it is not as simple as that. It also encompasses the shift of focus from blurred to sharp again, and for the world we know and recognise to change from monochrome back to full glorious technicolour.

Even in the stultifying presence of the fog, I felt that there was an important sequence playing out in my mind during this journey and I tried to accommodate it. There is something quite liberating about making a long car journey on your own – I find it therapeutic in the sense that I can give my emotional brain free rein; that part of my mind which is not concentrating on driving from A to B can flit about, wherever it chooses. There is a great deal to be said for uninterrupted solitude when it is chosen. I like the juxtaposition of the monotony of the road and the unexpected twists and turns of my thought processes; often a whole train of thought can be sparked by the name on the side of a lorry, or a village shop that I pass ... all manner of things can be triggers.

I drove out of the fog suddenly, after about thirty miles, and after such a long time, it was like driving into a different day. The sun shone out of a cerulean sky and houses, trees, fields ... all looked especially vibrant and colourful. My spirits were lifted by the beauty of the surroundings and the horrors of the fog receded with each passing mile. The return to normality was indeed a gift to all my senses.

Finally, the gift of silence is precious. It may seem strange to include it as a gift of loss, but there are times when you need to really connect with silence to feel at peace. Solitude can offer its own gifts, allowing you to focus on your thoughts around your particular loss. There is a singular beauty in being far enough away timewise from your loss to be able to choose when to tap into your thoughts. They can be picked up and examined and put down again without the wrenching pain that accompanies early loss.

This happened to me on a visit to a small hilltop village called Monagri, near Limassol in Cyprus.

Inside the sacred space of Monagri's plain little church, I experienced a special silence.

Gazing at an ancient painting of Madonna and child, their patrician faces expressing calm serenity, as I breathed in a hint of incense from years and days past, I felt that here I was in a truly spiritual place.

Though the painting was ornate with gold leaf, the overall simplicity of its message shone through.

There is no greater unconditional exchange of love than that which exists between mother and child. The continuum of daughters becoming mothers and their daughters in turn carrying on the blended family groups that are created line upon line is our history; it is our past, present and future.

In Monagri, I lit a slender tallow candle and set it amongst a few others in the simple container of sand. The flame flickered in the still air and the smoky scent drifted up my silent prayers to the ceiling and beyond.

The silence was absolute.

Silent is an anagram of listen.

In the silence, I listened.

In the stillness I heard ... only peace.

Sometimes we need to pare down to the nub to get to the profound truth, and I felt neither happy nor sad. I felt equable, balanced, strong, loved and loving. My heartbeat slowed, my breath was even and quiet.

I felt like a mother and a daughter.

I felt utterly content in the gift of the moment.

It is virtually impossible for us to find silence today, with the clamour of everyday life ruling our every move. From the electronic tones of our mobile phones to the cacophony of different tunes in every store in the shopping mall, we are constantly surrounded by man-made noise. Our devices talk to us, our computers bleep at us, even our household appliances beep and flash lights at us. At night, even when all the lights are out, there is a subtle hum of background noise that never seems to stop. It often feels as though it is beyond our control.

My moment of silence in Cyprus was precious for its rarity and its ability to stop me in my tracks and connect with the gifts I felt that I was being given. Discovering the purity of that moment's silence in that sacred space, feels to me like a Divine connection. In birth there is joy, in life there is challenge, in loss there is the hardest trial, but love transcends everything, and the true meaning of the gifts in it all is there for us to access if we want, and to share in the greatest love that supports, nurtures and sustains us throughout our lives.

I am reminded of the start of the 1920s prose poem by Max Erhmann, Desiderata: *Go placidly amid the noise and haste and remember what peace there may be in silence.*

Perhaps the most important of grief's gifts is the ability to listen … not only to yourself, but also to others, and ultimately to the silence that accompanies introspection, which enables you to learn from your pain, hold it, share it, let it out and thus help to heal others.

The most tangible shared gifts in my loss are the ability to share my feelings through writing, speaking and imagery. But the other, less visible gifts are equally important – the gift of knowing that pain can and does lessen, the storehouse gift of memories and the strength, comfort, safety, security and resilience that I have around me. Harnessing any or all of these positive attributes can and does allow the process of grieving to evolve in a committed and positive way for the future.

A letter to the Author

Dear Andrea

Someone suggested to me the other day that I write you a letter. It would be a 'good thing,' they said, and you would definitely benefit from it. Well, I know you pretty well, and suggesting that anything is a 'good thing' is sufficient to put you off, but I am hoping that you will stick with me and read to the end.

This won't be a letter of mincing words, of pussyfooting around the truth. No, it is going to be frank and hard-hitting as words on the page sometimes need to be, to get to the crux of it all. Just think of it as my gift to you.

So, Andrea, how are you doing?

No, I don't mean you to look at me with a half-smile and say, *"Oh, I am just fine ..."*

I am asking you to truly tell me, honestly, how you are doing.

You may wonder why I ask. It is because I really want to know how you are living with your unchosen status of bereaved parent.

There's no point dressing this up.

At the start, you will tell me it is Hideous with a capital H. It is unimaginably traumatic.

It is truly a living nightmare when your heart feels as though it has shattered into a million pieces, you might say.

It does not matter how your child lost his or her life, what age he or she was, what the particular circumstances were; all you want to do is wail and turn back the clock to the time before it happened.

But you can't.

But what you can do, and what I know you have learned

217

as you have gone along, may surprise some people. You have found, like others before you, that if you take it one step at a time and if you hold close the belief that you will survive what is arguably the greatest loss of all; you will garner the strength and motivation to move forward and emerge a stronger, more compassionate person.

I was pretty impressed, Andrea, with how you handled it to start with and how you have continued to handle it.

You have grown in empathy, soul and spirit in the years since that truly terrible late July day.

How have you managed to do it?

From the outside looking in, I see someone who is brave and strong. But you *hate* being called brave … and I know that is because you say, *"No, I am not brave. I had no choice but to get on with it after James died, trying at the same time to absorb this massive shock to the system."*

Other people's expectations can be a pressure in themselves and I recognise that you had to learn to side-line what everyone else wanted or needed you to do in favour of what your own instinct was telling you to do.

Parenting doesn't come with a rule book, nor does living in a world that has tilted on its axis. How are you expected to react?

I remember you saying, a while after James died,

"I can't walk down the high street smiling, you know. Because, people will

218

think, 'There goes that woman whose son died. What can she be smiling about?'

So you see, I have to adopt this neutral kind of mask, because it is what is expected of me. Friends and colleagues are always on tenterhooks. There's a certain kind of wary look they give you in case you start crying. So they don't really ask you any more how you are feeling, how you are coping. They just find it easier to pretend you are the same as you were before, very quickly after loss, and sometimes it is just simpler to take your lead from them. But I know that made me seem cold and defensive."

Well, you say that, but you had to protect yourself while the grief was still that sharp jagged thing digging into you all the time like a stitch.

How else could you cope?

It is only with the benefit of hindsight that you can see how 'difficult' you were to be around. It is only now, too, that people are brave enough to tell you how awkward you were. But you shouldn't need to apologise for being defensive when you were in a place that is so difficult to negotiate.

One of the problems you faced when you presented your mask of neutrality to the world is that you still had to deal with the turbulent emotions. It is all very well to pack your grief into a box and clamp it shut, but you learned the hard way that you have to take off the lid sometimes, lest the sorrow seeps out, or worse, bursts out when you least expect it.

You were ultimately quite sensible with this, and found safe, controlled ways to visit and share your grief through examining it and talking about it.

You guarded against getting stuck in negativity by consciously seeking out the positives wherever you could find them. You actively looked for gifts. And you began to find them.

You haven't run out of words yet, have you? You know you are lucky to have the gift of expression and that can be utilised to help others. The creativity is in part fuelled by the appreciation of those who read your words and benefit from them.

The publication of *Into the Mourning Light* was the culmination of eight years of gathering together many helpful and uplifting words.

Now you have completed this, your second book.

You tell me how much easier it is now to write of your loss, because you have told the most personal of stories and the grief has softened to a more malleable and manageable level.

Your writing is an ongoing legacy for James, and it gives purpose, meaning and reason to sharing and analysing common thoughts around the issues of loss and mourning. And your voice, well! - how that has developed. You have always been a thinker and a talker, though never such a public one, and when opportunities arise for you to speak of your mourning path you take to them with a new confidence.

You are a grief achiever.

I know too, that all the things you do to share your mourning are in honour of your son's memory. Of course! All you ever want as a parent is to be proud of your children and for them to be proud of you. Why shouldn't that pride still be there and grow?

I appreciate that you still have times of self-doubt. I sense that in the dark hours you long for someone to come and take that terrible pain of loss away and you weep for the future that James cannot have, all that promise of his life gone in an instant.

You have cried out at the unfairness of it, the injustice of his lost future, to faith, to spirit, to God. These days, I think, you begin to understand a little more that the elements of hope, love, light, faith and resilience are sustaining you in ways you never imagined.

In regard to how your grief has evolved, you say this,

"I had this horrible inner rage that had to be balanced out by seeking out something positive to come from my loss, despite my heartfelt longing not to have to make this constant effort, this searching all the time, for meaning and sense from what has happened. Working through my grief on my own terms

is key to my being able to share how I have done it. I am not saying my way is the best way, or the only way, just that it works for me and if it helps others along similar routes, that is a source of joy."

So, there you are, Andrea. I believe this letter has turned out to be a good thing after all, charting as it does the progress you have made and continue to make along a route which was never planned.

Keep on keeping on and I will write again soon …

Chapter 9
Keys

Remember

Remember me when I am gone away
Gone far away into the silent land:
When you can no more hold me by the hand
Nor I half turn to go, yet turning stay
Remember me when no more day by day
You tell me of our future that you planned
Only remember me; you understand
It will be late to counsel then or pray
Yet if you should forget me for a while
And afterwards remember; do not grieve
For if the darkness and corruption leave
A vestige of the thoughts that once I had
Better by far you should forget and smile,
Than that you should remember and be sad.

This poem, written by Christina Rossetti in the 1800s[1], holds a universal relevance to loss. It is equally applicable to the passing of a mother, friend, child or spouse. The beauty of the words is emphasised by the constant prompts to remember which run like a refrain throughout the sonnet. At the time the poem was written, the process of mourning was in many ways far more public and visible than it is today; much was written about it in this rather pensive and tentative style.

Given the quaintness of the archaic language, the sentiments remain viable on a day when we are likely to be visiting our own personal losses.

Mother's Day is a day that fuses joy and poignancy in equal mix. I always remember my late mum fondly, but particularly so on Mother's Day. Though she died in 2001, quite a while ago now, I could never *forget her and smile* as Rossetti suggests, rather I *remember her, and smile*.

That would be my hope for anyone who is mourning their mum, whether the loss is recent or longer ago.

Reminiscing, examining and holding fond memories are some of the best ways to recall a loving and much-loved mum.

A mum who is firm but fair, who can be a best friend as well as a mother, a role model, supporter, tear-wiper, empathiser, nurturer and teacher – those of us who have - or had - mothers like this are indeed fortunate.

And when these very special mums have left us, what else is there to do but to draw in that distinctive, maternal love and make it ours? Then we can share it with our nearest and dearest. It is a joy to pour the love that our mothers have given us onto our husbands, siblings, children, friends. We keep the memories of our mum alive by paying forward all that love they showered on us in their lifetime. We smile and laugh fondly in our remembering. I remember too how becoming a mother myself taught me so much about my own mum. Suddenly I had parental responsibility for the gift of new, precious life and from mum's experience she knew exactly how that would make me feel.

Loving and supportive, she was always there for me with advice, guidance, humour and affection. If there were exams for being a good mum to my brother and me, our mum would have passed with flying colours.

I have been blessed with two wonderful children, and despite losing James, I remain the mother of two wonderful children.

Stella and I always mark Mother's Day though it is poignant with memory for both of us.

Stella is now a happily married mum herself, not only to Charlie born in 2014, but also to Grace, her beautiful daughter who was born in December 2016.

Mother's Day celebrations are not limited to mums and daughters, either. Boys can give their mums flowers too – as an older teen, James invariably managed to find a last-minute bouquet, though it's fair to say he usually borrowed the funds to buy it! It's easy to sanctify him now, but his heart was in the right place and the love and affection he held for his family and friends was never in doubt.

My Stella shines in her own right, like a bright star in my maternal constellation, just as James does, even though he is no longer with us.

And now Stella and I are so lucky to have the wonderful continuum of life as grandmother, mother and daughter to celebrate. Becoming a grandmother to my daughter and stepdaughter's children brings me great joy and I love my extended maternal role.

In *Into the Mourning Light*, Stella reflected that she would miss her brother's presence especially on her wedding day and when she had her own children. Now that both these wonderful life events have happened, I wondered how she feels, in retrospect. She says,

"It's the milestones that get me: All those special dates and life events that should be celebrated with James, so maddeningly thrown away in one, careless moment, and each one is another kick, another reminder of what – or who – I'm missing.

After losing our Dad at a relatively young age (I was 19, James was 16 – it happened just over 2.5 years before we lost James), I just assumed that James would one day walk me down the aisle, towards my mystical groom. Wistfully, I imagined him walking proudly at my side; me holding on to him for reassurance, him giving me a huge James smile and subtly squeezing my arm to spur me on towards the happy future standing ahead of me, with familiar expressions and mannerisms, reminiscent of our dad, whose shoes he would be wearing metaphorically on that special day.

I met my lovely husband Pete a mere two weeks before James died. Talk about a challenging start! The poor guy was only just beginning to get to know me then, suddenly he was catapulted into the unenviable role usually given to those who best know us; to support me through, no doubt, the worst time in my life and the grief that followed (and continues to follow). Shortly after receiving that awful phone call from Mum one sunny Sunday morning in July ("Stella, it's the worst news..."), Pete asked me what I wanted him to do, and I gave him an easy get-out clause; I told him to do whatever he wanted to do, and said that I had to focus on what had just happened and what was to happen next. He told me he wanted to stay and be there for me – so he did, and 14 years later we're married with two beautiful children!

How cruel a twist life took, though. How unfair that on the happiest day of my life, there was a James-shaped hole where his spirit and smile used to shine so brightly.

The honour of walking me down the aisle was bestowed upon my wonderful stepdad and he carried out his role with pride. Of course, I had a wonderful day, but it pains me even now to allow myself to think about how it 'should' have been; James taking the role of proud brother and Usher alongside Pete's best friends and his brother-in-law. James would have loved our wedding day. In the evening, we had a brilliantly cheesy band and everyone enjoyed singing along and dancing – he would have been in his element!

Just over a year later, we welcomed Charlie into the world and in a very swift but significant period of metamorphosis (not that it felt swift at the time!) I became a mother. Suddenly, life all made sense: My inner lioness had stirred,

227

and I knew innately that it was down to me to protect, to nurture, to love him with all of my being. I remember, in the crazy haze of those sleepless new-born days, I would spend so much time just staring at him, studying him as he lay sleeping in my arms, wondering how I could have possibly been so lucky to be blessed with my own son.

At times, however, I couldn't stop my mind from wandering completely, to the dark caverns of fear and worry within my mind (one of the many unwelcome side effects of grief – the constant worry that someone else you love will die when you least expect it); I had an underlying fear of my bubble bursting, of my happiness being destroyed in one instant – much as it had been when we lost James. My greatest dread, like many parents, is of losing a child, and an ominous shadow hangs over me if I allow it to; the feeling of my happiness being too good to be true is real, and I think having an awareness more heightened than most, of what such a catastrophic bereavement would be like, means I truly fear it. I still have to work hard not to let my mind get carried away, from marring otherwise happy times with my children in the present.

Having seen Mum go through the long, winding, confusing and intermingling paths of grief since losing James, I know that it really is as bad as you could ever imagine. Her approach to embracing her grief and moving forward with it is incredibly admirable, yet I know that it is always an uphill struggle. We've spoken before about both feeling that we're 'bored of this game now' and felt like we had proved (to who? I don't know…) that we could 'cope', but we couldn't be bothered anymore! It is a perpetual, evolving process, ebbing and flowing like the tide and lapping against the shores of our minds. Handling grief 'well' isn't an accolade either of us ever wished to be given, despite all the lovely supportive words we have heard from loved ones and acquaintances over the years.

I've found out the hard way myself that, when a key accomplishment in your life is coping with a significant loss such as losing a sibling at a young age, mentioning it in passing in a new social situation tends to kill a conversation pretty quickly. This is especially the case when those who don't run away at the first sentence tend to ask probing questions that lead me to divulge that, yes, I hadn't long lost my father too! Much easier to be able to wax lyrical about sporting awards or career successes, I'm sure.

Being a mother to Charlie, and also his little sister, Grace who is just over 2 years younger, is now one of my greatest achievements, and one that I am always happy to wax lyrical about! I don't always get it right (does anyone?) but I am sure that they have every ounce of love and devotion that I can afford to give them from my bursting heart – and then some! I love watching their developing interactions with each other and I take joy in seeing so much of James's character (and fleeting facial expressions) in Charlie, as I remember him from our own childhood. How I wish he were here to enjoy being Uncle James: he would have delightfully relished his title and I have no doubt that the children would have adored him. We talk about Uncle James with Charlie (now 5) and he loves to hear stories that I can recall about growing up with him and the adventures we went on! It's lovely to have the opportunity to reignite the flames of those lovely memories, so often extinguished by the gravity of loss and kept in a dusty box for years, in favour of dwelling on the negatives.

Becoming a mother has helped me to draw a faint line under my grief, a new chapter I suppose – one where I am officially a grown-up and have my own line to carve. It still lives alongside me and pops up at unexpected times to upset my inner equilibrium, but it is mostly diluted now by my confidence in the future that I plan to have with my little family. I am not about to 'cherish every moment' as I think it creates a lot of pressure in an already pressurised life (and, frankly, some moments are better off forgotten!), but I am learning to cherish the delightful moments; to cherish their tiny, sticky little hands, and to be grateful for being needed by my two babies in a way that only a mother can be."

These wonderful words only serve to underline how a mother's status is undoubtedly underrated as the life-affirming and responsible position that it is. Mothers put their children first without question. As a mum, you instantly become unselfish – yet you hold selfishly to the joys of babyhood, cherishing the memories of your children's early responses to your loving.

You treasure every little piece of love that your child gives you and reflect it, bouncing it back to them without any forethought.

The bond that is formed between you in those early days is never broken. Your children remain your babies, and they stay part of you forever.

Even when you lose your child and you grieve; you grieve with love as well as sorrow.

You grieve with regret for the future that your child cannot have but you also grieve with loving memories of the time that you had together, however short that may have been.

Moving forward as a mother after you have lost a child is a massive challenge.

You question your abilities as a mother, you even question your right to be a mother.

You cannot help feeling that you must have failed in some way for your child to die.

You would bargain anything if it would only give you back your child.

But slowly, the guilt lessens, the sadness becomes absorbed and you discover the keys that grief has given you to cope with this new life. You acquire a new, loving kind of wisdom, a new vision for looking forward. Though there is nothing to forgive, ultimately you feel forgiven.

When you lose a child, other mothers are filled with fear of how they would manage if this unimaginable thing happened to them.

Instead of dwelling on that, I exhort all mothers to dwell on the love they have for their children, not their fear of living without them.

As bereaved parents, the loss of your children does not lessen your maternal love; rather it intensifies it into new directions and takes you to places you could never have imagined.

Motherhood is not only biological; it can also be spiritual. Many people looking for a maternal figure can turn to those who may not be blood relatives, but they too can share in that special kind of guiding love; it is truly love without bounds.

In remembering, we rejoice in the power of maternal love, the sheer joy of loving unconditionally and being loved in return.

Eleanor Roosevelt said,[2] 'You gain strength, courage and confidence by every experience in which you really stop to look fear in the face. You are able to say to yourself, *'I have lived through this horror. I can take the next thing that comes along. You must do the thing you think you cannot do.'*'

I am borrowing her idea of keys because I think they are important markers in how you perceive your own progress in grieving. I would say there are a finite number of keys to living with loss and these, my own observations, are but a sample.

Strength is inherent in us, but it is undoubtedly fed by our life experiences. My mother used to say, *"what doesn't kill you makes you stronger"* and I believe that strength and resilience in the face of adversity help you to cope with whatever has happened in the past, what you are going through now, and what lies ahead. I find that conserving strength by taking a step back from difficulties seems to consolidate innate strength into something even more powerful. Grief, guilt and loss sap strength on a daily basis and it is tiring work. It is important to be kind to yourself when you are feeling feeble to empower yourself to carry on. And being kind to yourself can take many forms – from simply indulging in your favourite chocolate to going on a meditative retreat (for example).

When James died, at first, I prayed simply for the strength to breathe, to continue to put one foot in front of the other and to keep on going. I am still standing – but it is not just strength that is responsible …

Courage and bravery go hand in hand.

Is courage the same as bravery? I don't particularly like being called brave.

I do not think I am especially brave. I do however think that I have the quality of spirit to face difficulties without feeling afraid of the consequences. I used to think that I was either rewarded or punished for how I live my life, but my faith and convictions have changed over the years so that I am closer to understanding how, although it can appear to be the case at times, none of us is singled out for specific joys or tragedies in life.

My courage allows me to speak out, to write, to share James with an ever-widening audience to bring awareness not only of the dangers inherent in water, but also the consequences of living with tragic loss. It is courage that allows me to confront the stark fact of loss, not to let it get the upper hand. I confess that I often see grief as an adversary to be beaten down and pummelled into submission, even though I am a pacifist at heart!

Confidence I never believed I had the confidence to address Kingston Council on the topic of river safety. I never believed I had the confidence to write and publish my first book *Into the Mourning Light,* let alone follow it up with this one. I never believed I had the confidence to share my personal story in presentations and with the media. I never believed I had the confidence to pitch articles to magazines or to write a blog.

All these things I have done, and I stand tall and proud of these achievements, which have emerged in spite of what is arguably the worst confidence sapper on earth.

Confidence feeds on itself and I am certain that outward confidence reflects the strength and courage that lie within.

Exploration Where does exploration fit here? By exploration, I mean investigating outside your comfort zone. In the early days of grief, the world is a dark and lonely place. But gradually … as you poke your head above the parapet you begin to get back your human urge to *explore* new horizons and investigate new directions. Embrace it, welcome it and use it. If you are drawn to do something reckless, as long as it is not overtly life-threatening, do it!

My favourite personal example of this is the irresistible urge I had to go paragliding when I was on holiday in Turkey in 2007, which I described in *Into the Mourning Light*. Jumping off that high point and taking flight was one of the greatest adrenaline rushes ever, and I felt closer to Heaven and James than ever before, whilst also having the courage to place my confidence in the ability of the paraglider pilot to keep us safe. I enjoyed the physical, emotional and spiritual experience so much I repeated it in the second week of our holiday. Exploration also encompasses learning and there is nothing quite like learning a new skill or acquiring a new qualification for boosting courage, confidence, strength and a sense of self-worth. Be selective and do what you want to do once in a while. It is innate in us to please others but sometimes it is ok to be *selfish* rather than *selfless* and most importantly, not to feel guilty about it.

Exploration happens when you can haul yourself out of the dark places and kick out apathy and passivity. Taking control is empowering in itself.

Hope When everything is dark and sad, when all seems to be conspiring against you to challenge, weaken, and destroy you, how then, do you find hope? As I wrote in Chapter 1, I believe that hope must be drawn around us like a protective cloak to become one of the first key elements that can move us forward in our pain and loss.

The enemy of hope is fear, and there is no more fearful place than early grief. The action of conquering fear and anxiety – which takes time and effort, motivates our hope for the future. Roosevelt's suggestion for overcoming fear is self-discipline--once you have faced certain fears, the strength and confidence gained from those experiences foster the overcoming of new fears.

My own return to hope came when I recognised that taking a proactive approach to grief worked far better for me than allowing myself to become mired in hopeless negatively. It was **so** hard in the beginning but the hopefulness that I began to feel, and the uplifting responses to my early writing efforts made me realise that I could do this dreadful thing and by sharing my story and James's story, feed on the hope and positive outcome from our personal tragedy.

My hope reflects a degree of interdependence; it is not just mine, and the more I share my hope, the greater my realisation that we need empathy, support, faith and understanding to move forward.

The return of hope to your life after loss and trauma is represented by a new sense of optimism and certainty that things will improve, that you can cope, and you have the ability to live life meaningfully again. You have to work at it, pray for it, and greet it with gratitude when it arrives. To go from *hopeless* to *hopeful* is a result of much hard work and diligent application. It remains a work in progress on a daily basis. Being filled with hope is akin to convalescing from an illness, day by day you realise you are a little stronger and a little better able to confront obstacles.

There is too a kind of symmetry and balance in hope that is well illustrated by Sheridan Voysey's view[3] that if we are emotionally fit, we have 'the ability to amplify positive emotions like peace, gratitude, hope or love, while managing negative ones like bitterness, sadness or anger.' In addition to the emotional and spiritual keys that we may use, there are practical actions which help with the day to day drudgery of grieving. Some of the suggestions which you can embrace are:

Do things for others

Grief, particularly soon after loss, is both solitary and introspective. The act of reaching out is not easily achievable. However, simply sharing as much of your own story as you wish to reveal with others in a similar situation is mutually therapeutic. You do not need to do things for others in the form of charitable acts, but simply communicate as best you can. Simple exchanges create positive outcomes for both parties.

Connect with people

When trauma strikes, you sometimes have to reassess your needs and accept interventions that you would otherwise reject.

I don't know where I would be today if it were not for the other bereaved parents whom I met, virtually and in reality, through The Compassionate Friends and Drowning Support Network. Both organisations provided a safe haven for me to share and explore my emotions from the early days. I also received support from CRUSE and whilst I was initially very defensive about 'talking therapy' for my loss, as time passed, I realised its benefit to my overall sense of wellbeing.

Take care of your body

Actually, I would extend this to say 'take care of your body and your mind' because a holistic approach encompassing mind, body and spirit is the most beneficial way to make you feel better about what has happened. If you are as fit as you are able to be, you are stronger and better placed to begin to shape a better future. Physical activity produces endorphins (the feel-good hormone) which in turn can boost immunity as well as lifting your spirits.

Notice the world around you

We are all so busy these days rushing from one point to another that it is easy to fail to take time to smell the roses.

If you utilise all your senses when you take a walk, it is virtually impossible <u>not</u> to feel uplifted by the world around you and take pleasure in, for example, the changing of the seasons. Buying fresh flowers for the kitchen windowsill is a simple way to introduce some everyday colour to your day and to bring to notice the natural world.

Keep learning new things

The thirst for knowledge can never be quenched. In experiencing loss, you may discover a very strong need to learn more about grief to try to understand how best to process it. Reading is one of the best tools for expanding knowledge. But you should not limit your learning to the topics closest to you.

Sometimes it is helpful to learn something entirely outside your comfort zone to stimulate interest, which then has a tangential knock on effect in making familiar targets seem more achievable, and easier.

Have goals to look forward to

In early grief the smallest aims seem incredible to achieve. Getting through a day hour by hour seems impossible at first. But slowly and surely you come to realise that with each day that passes you feel minutely better. Goals such as being able to enjoy going out without feeling guilty are not achieved overnight – but they are achievable. Today my goals relate to living mindfully, joyfully and meaningfully in spite of my loss.

Find ways to bounce back

It is true to say that we all have a story. Few of us swan through life without experiencing trauma, loss or sadness. But we all possess untapped reserves of optimism and strength that together provide us with the resilience to manage tough times. By focusing on what we actually can achieve, rather than having unrealistic expectations, we can grow stronger. Putting together a toolbox to manage adversity is a useful device. My own toolbox contains mindfulness, writing, reading, art, talking, walking, spiritual nourishment, amongst other things.

Take a positive approach

The concept of looking for anything positive in loss seems counterproductive. However, your efforts to be proactive in grieving pay massive dividends in providing a positive platform from which to launch your future. Losing my son is the worst thing that has happened in my life. Yet I am still here, still standing, still upright and still making a useful contribution to life.

It is only by constantly focusing on the positive aspects of my life – my loving husband, family and friends that I am able to put into perspective the tragic loss we have experienced. Turning negativity into positivity means looking for the light that comes after the darkness. And it does come ... in the way that day follows night.

Be comfortable with who you are

When we are young, we are inclined to measure ourselves against others and find ourselves wanting in some way or another – that's human nature. But maturity brings with it a certain degree of self-acceptance. You must not beat yourself up over things that have happened in the past and which you cannot change. A level of self-assurance is undoubtedly helpful in traversing the grief road. Experiencing loss gives you a greater ability to present a face to the world that says, *take me as I am. This is who I am today.* I am (finally) comfortable in my own skin.

Be part of something bigger

As individual human beings we are all part of the *something bigger* that is humanity, but it is within the bounds of our circle of family, friends, work and the community to which we belong that we tread our own paths.

Making a difference as an individual can appear difficult to achieve but we only have to look at the efforts, of, say, a fund-raiser running a marathon for a given charity, to see that we all have it in us, in some form or another, to be part of something bigger. Any creative strength and spreading the word, through writing or speaking, creates a sense of being part of a wider community and adding to the knowledge base of others.

For myself, the satisfaction of being part of something bigger - in grief terms - is being able to share the path of my sorrow with an ever-widening audience and at the same time as helping others in grief and loss, help myself towards a better understanding and assimilation of loss.

We all need to feel that we are here for a purpose. Sometimes it is hard to see exactly what that purpose is, and anything that helps towards clarity is a useful tool, not just in grieving but in our day to day living.

It is difficult to convey the sense of wellbeing that has its roots in our innermost soul, at the very heart of us. This is the nebulous sense of joy that does not come from external stimuli, or our daily circumstances, but is an inbuilt emotion that we can draw upon if we are lucky enough to be able to recognise, identify and embrace it. Joy arrives when the keys of successfully dealing with grief open the door to a new happiness.

A return to joy from the depths of grieving is a hard won and long struggle that remains a work in progress. The return of joy after loss makes me think of approaching a building project, brick by brick. It starts small, with the foundation level being the first instance when you recognise an awareness of positive emotion affecting how you feel.

You feel happy.

You don't feel guilty about feeling happy.

You hold on to the feeling, drinking in the emotion that surrounds you and fold it into your heart.

You have one of those lightbulb moments. This can be built on!

Gradually the bricks mould into something more substantial.

Events which please, be they small or significant, begin to form something solid on which to lean, a structure that becomes denser and supportive so that you not only feel joy, you have the confidence and assurance to begin to give out that joy to others.

The conviction that life is getting better and growing happier again, despite what you have lost, is a source of ever strengthening joy. It is supported by the love of those around you. As you give out the light of your joy, so it is reflected back to you.

Joy is often bittersweet because you need to have known pain to recognise the beauty that lies within the joy which comes later. Each of us knows this in very disparate ways. Personally, I think that joy comes most from the knowledge that I am loved. I believe that in my insignificance as just another human being on the planet, somewhere in the massive universe, I actually matter.

And that faith brings its own form of un-diminishable joy; it is the joy that makes me want to keep on living, keep on learning and keep on exploring life's great adventure. It's an extension, an elaboration and a significantly deep addition to the initial hesitant progress in grief.

When you think about it, we all possess two things that work separately but in harmony with each other. They have an interdependent relationship for neither can survive without the other. I am referring to the brain and the heart.

The brain is a complex organ constructed to perform myriad functions, whilst the heart is in effect a simpler affair, working efficiently as a muscle and a pump, literally pumping iron night and day. Its four chambers are the powerhouse for all our life blood.

The steady rhythm of our mother's heartbeat is the first sound we ever hear.

There is an expression that is popular in the context of an approach to faith: 'head knowledge and heart knowledge.' Head knowledge can be described as gathering information prosaically, akin to learning by rote. Heart knowledge is more about revelation, those lightbulb moments when you say, *"Ahh, now I understand. Now I really get it!"* and this is well applied to the study of works of faith such as the Bible.

Further, head knowledge relates to our capacity for learning, while heart knowledge is about the wisdom gained from life experiences, both good and bad.

Following on from this, I imagined how the brain and heart might discuss how they cope with grief.

Heart begins, *"I am aching with loss. I am broken, fractured … I have to work just as hard as usual, but I am tired. I am sick. How can I ever recover?"*

Brain replies, *"Yes, I already know you are in a dark place. So am I. I cannot get away from constantly playing and replaying events. I am not only living every day in grief; I am constantly thinking about grief and sadness too. I am a DVD stuck on a loop. Round and round we go; it is just so exhausting!"*

Heart says, *"Well, it's OK for you. You can switch off when you want to. I can't do that. Even though I am broken, I have to work the same way as I did before, powering on regardless. I am the one who is stuck on a treadmill."*

"You talk of switching off?" Brain retorts. *"In your dreams, Heart. This loss is with me every second of every day. Awake or asleep, I have to deal with triggers, memories, sights, sounds and scents, all of which conspire to remind me of that which I have lost. All you need to do is to keep on pumping. Huh!"*

"Keep on pumping, you really think that is all I do?" (Heart is beating faster now). *"Just remember Brain, that I am the repository for love, affection, emotion and personality. I can melt at a kind word or cry at a sharp retort. If you think about it, I am the one who holds the key to the soul, not you."*

Brain is quiet for a moment, considering this. *"Ah yes, but just remember, that without my intellect to process what you do, you wouldn't even know your purpose. Ha, what have you got to say to that?"*

Heart heaves a sigh and triple beats for a few seconds.
"You think you are so clever Brain, don't you? And I guess you are. But it is only when your facts reach me, when I process them into feelings and sentiments, that there is any benefit. Together we create something that is more spiritual than prosaic."

Brain replies, *"The bottom line is that we need each other to sift, process and balance the knowledge that comes our way. And we need one another to pull together through those dark moments when we can't see the light. We need to acknowledge our sadness and use our disparate abilities to press on forward. That's how we can deal with this."*

"And I am there for you, Brain, in the quiet of the night when you need a hug, you know that don't you? I can flutter, I can beat, I can race, and I can just quietly potter along in the background for you. I can be whatever you need at any given time. You only have to say."

"I hear you, dear Heart," says brain finally. *"I guess we are in this together for the long haul, then."*

"Yes," replies Heart, *"until it is decreed that it is time for us to stop working then we will both take our onward journey side by side, do you agree?"*

Brain replies with a single word. *"Symbiosis."*

And they settle comfortably into silence.

Head knowledge and heart knowledge are equally important in an approach to living successfully and fruitfully after loss. My head knowledge of loss is practical, prosaic

246

and down to earth. My heart knowledge is made up from memories, stitched together with love. In the end, it is love that is the most important key of all.

Chapter 10
Resilience

He did not say you will not be storm tossed, you will not be sore distressed, you will not be work weary. He said ... you will not be overcome.
Julian of Norwich[1]

Julian of Norwich was, in fact, a woman. She was an early Christian mystic, who lived a virtually hermitic life and wrote much about the privations and trials of life in the 14th century. Julian lived in a time of turmoil, but her theology was optimistic, and this is reflected in her writing. She promoted a message of hope and the certainty of being loved.

Despite her pared down existence which was about as minimalist as life could be, Julian of Norwich possessed the grit and resilience required to carry on in the face of the obstacles of the way she lived.

Resilience is harder to live than it is to quantify; it is our innate ability to bounce back after we have been flattened by life events. We will have been changed beyond all recognition, yet we manage to come out on the other side. Many will remember the 1977 science fiction film, *Close Encounters of the Third Kind,* written and directed by Steven Spielberg. It tells the story of an ordinary man whose life changes in extraordinary ways after an encounter with an unidentified flying object.

Every parent who loses a child is catapulted from a hitherto ordinary to an extraordinary world - in the true sense of the word. Trying to acclimatise to the unwanted, unfamiliar planet of grief is a massive challenge.

Over time, my grief planet has become more like home. I have learned to negotiate the terrain that at first looked like an alien, un-mapped space. My grief Satnav has charted the blind alleys, the no through roads, the cul-de-sacs and finally the multi-lane highways with the occasional diversion that reflect a slipping back into distress, triggered by differing outside forces.

The storms that once blocked the routes have given way to sunshine, clouds, light breezes with the occasional shower, and many rainbows.

In *Close Encounters*, Richard Dreyfuss's character feels a connection he cannot sever with the UFO. The subliminal images that plague him throughout the film remind me of how, in the early days of loss, memories play repeatedly across the mind's eye like inescapable screensavers on an endless loop.

You can neither turn off your memories nor eliminate your shock at the fact that this person whom you love so much is no longer physically here, and what you have left is a flat line, static level of memories, like an album of images to which you cannot add.

Accepting that your life cannot have a neatly tied up ending like a fictional story or screenplay is tough.

I find that time has unfolded the gift that loss has gradually offered: it has led to numerous new connections which in turn form fresh memories that include James, albeit in a more ethereal sense.

In 2016 I was asked to speak at a public event at the RNLI College, the organisation's headquarters in Poole, Dorset. The event was a fish-themed fundraising evening hosted by the RNLI to launch the charity's annual Fish Supper Campaign.

My talks and presentations are generally based on living with bereavement and loss. They have been tailored to groups who are either grieving or connected with the grieving. This time, I was asked to engage with an audience of around 80 people, at a reasonably light-hearted social event. Those attending were connected with the RNLI and also included members of the public who had purchased tickets for the advertised event.

I thought about the brief; it presented something of a challenge to ensure that I did not bring down the tone of what should be an enjoyable, relaxed evening.

I needed to tell James's story in a way that would ultimately provide positive messages.

I decided to base my presentation around the theme of connections. As mentioned, my new connections started very soon after James died in 2005, through our work with Kingston council. Our ultimately successful three-year campaign was a gratifying legacy for James in its own right. Through connections that I made over that time and beyond, I talked at CRUSE bereavement training days and co-presented workshops at the Harry Edwards Healing Sanctuary. Connections with the US Based Drowning Support Network also led to more writing and friendships made across the water – and across the ether.

As previously described, I told James's story for the RNLI's Respect the Water campaign in 2014 and was heavily involved in the campaign that year, amongst other things in composing the text for the beer glasses supplied in local pubs and restaurants.

This turned out to be one of the best, but one of the hardest things I have had to do. Variants of the text were shown to a focus group to assess their impact. When the RNLI's Ross told me that the text telling James's personal story was the text that would be used, I felt like crying but I realised just how important the telling of our personal story is to emphasise the impact of what has happened; and as a preventative measure for the future.

I have no shortage of material and I structured my

presentation around the connections I've made and the positive aspects of life after loss. I illustrated the talk with slides which chronicled the key events. At the event, the MC introduced me as an '*Ambassador for the Respect the Water campaign*', an accolade which makes my heart swell with pride – naturally, on my son's behalf.

When I choose to give voice to and share what has come from living with loss, it is always done from the heart and in loving memory of James.

I chose not to dwell on grief and loss per se, except for two key points which I hoped the audience would take home with them.

Firstly, I asked that people do not turn away from the grieving because they 'don't know what to say.' How much better it is ... to say a few carefully chosen words than cross to the other side of the street in avoidance.

And I made the point that offering help should be tangible, rather than an open *"let me know if there is anything I can do,"* which puts someone on the spot. The newly bereaved are not good decision makers; it is as much as they can do to put one foot in front of the other.

Secondly, although it is your natural inclination to try, you should resist the urge to empathise. It's no use telling me that you understand how I feel because your pet was put down last week (yes that really did happen to me). Better to say nothing at all!

I concluded my talk with a quote from Jimmy Carter, former President of the USA[2]. At the time I paraphrased it to remove the reference to faith and applied it to each and every person associated with the RNLI. But it definitely echoes my own mind set in dealing with grief today:

"I have one life and one chance to make it count for something... My faith demands that I do whatever I can, wherever I am, whenever I can, for as long as I can with whatever I have to try to make a difference."

Afterwards, two members of the audience came to me. *"Thank you,"* said a tall man, his eyes heavy with tears. He clasped my hand in both his and said, *"You really struck a chord with your words. I won't forget them."* And he turned and walked away, leaving me wondering what it was in particular that had resonated with him to such a degree. Another woman approached me, and simply said, *"I'm a mum. Can I give you a hug?"* She folded me into her embrace and despite the emotion, I felt heartened at these two demonstrations of empathy. Being public in my grief brings with it a vulnerability and the potential of being judged by my actions. I am lucky that I meet largely with positive responses.

The fact is that the RNLI organisation recognises and understands connections.

None of us can ever forget that tragic accidental loss of

life impacts on and reverberates through many lives, whenever, however and wherever it happens.

Whatever I can do to help lessen these effects reflects my heartfelt desire to stress the importance of understanding how careful we must all be around water; however innocuous it may appear.

We must do this in order to prevent further traumatic loss to individuals, the emergency services, and ordinary families such as mine; who never wanted to be extraordinary. Something - be it faith, strength, support of family and friends, or a combination of all these, give us the resilience and determination to bring something positive out of the hideously negative.

I have met many inspirational people following the loss of James. One of these is Jackie Roberts, whose daughter Megan died in horribly similar circumstances. We met through shared representation on the National Water Safety Forum. Jackie went on to work with the Royal Life Saving Society and her strength, courage and resilience brought a new emphasis to the organisation's work to reduce drowning fatalities. Jackie contributes here her personal story surrounding the loss of her Megan and how her resilience has helped her through the trauma of loss.

"Looking back now, five years on, it's difficult for me to fathom just how I survived the initial shock of realising that Megan, my beautiful, funny,

ethereal daughter, was nowhere. No one knew where she was.

It was January 2014 and the weekend had been one of working (I was involved with a horse livery yard at the time where the physically demanding work had helped me deal with the aftermath of having breast cancer) and getting soaked to the skin because of the weather.

A message from her friend Bethanie reached me at some early hour on a Monday morning. Though even now I can't bear to read it, to check the wording, it said something along the lines of 'I don't want to worry you, but we are wondering if Megan is at home in Wetherby as none of us have had any replies from her over the weekend and we start uni lectures again tomorrow. (Bethanie sent it on Sunday night)

My initial reaction had been one of cold dread; swiftly followed by rational thought: she must have gone to see her ex-boyfriend. That relationship was one that she still held on to, despite all her attempts to let him go.

That Monday morning I also had the strong feeling that I'd been thrown into the plot of a strange horror story, as I panicked; called my brother; called the police, didn't know whether to worry my parents at this stage; called my other brother; let my work colleague know I had a problem so I wouldn't be at work that morning; called Megan's ex-boyfriend (who hadn't seen her since Christmas apparently) and felt, throughout all this, that Megan was trying to tell me where she was. Maybe that was a sign of resilience even at the start. I was panicking but some little used, primeval, part of my brain somehow kept me walking, talking and communicating, even though I don't believe I was entirely present in my own body.

As the day went on, our lovely old house became full of people, followed by days of media invasion, with reporters knocking on the door, then more people arriving and messages from so many people I lost count and eventually the news that we didn't want to hear. We received confirmation from the police that our worst fears were quite possibly correct, and Megan had somehow fallen into the river Ouse.

Megan's last known sighting on CCTV, on the night that her friends last remember seeing her, showed her, heavily influenced by alcohol, turning right just before Lendal Bridge in York. Her female friend and two of the boys in the group had reached the bridge by this point, on their way to McDonald's. Unfortunately, Megan had become left behind and without realizing where she was heading, followed the third male, who turned before the bridge and ran down in front of a pub called the Maltings, in the direction of the river. Megan could be seen on the far side of the walkway, opposite the pub, stumbling into cycle racks. Shortly after this, the young male could be seen on the pub's CCTV footage, running back up past the camera whilst Megan, in her flimsy flowery dress and flat pumps, didn't reappear.

It took the police some time to piece it all together but it appeared that none of the group had been aware that Megan was even with them, let alone had gone missing; she had quietly disappeared into the darkness under Lendal Bridge and, as we discovered for sure months later, due to further evidence, she had fallen into the river from some treacherous open steps at the foot of the bridge. Somehow, as the days became weeks, my mind and body kept functioning. I don't know how, but I was filled with what I can only describe as an energy that made me feel almost superhuman at times ... all my emotions on overload and my mind somehow staying calm and rational. I felt determined to hold it all together for everyone, to keep my other children, Amy and Ben, safe and grounded and to not burden all my friends and family with the absolute horror that was fuelling my strange surreal state. I felt the strongest umbilical pull from my stomach the day that the police took me to one side to confirm that she had last been seen near the river. I had to pass on this information to my children, my other family and my ex in-laws who were all waiting in the dining room and they all cried. As they cried, I just stopped crying. I couldn't cry. My father-in-law was hugging me and said: 'Let it all out Jackie' but I wasn't ready to do that. I was Megan's mum and I couldn't give up as first of all we had to find her and secondly, if I continued crying, I might never have stopped.

It was six weeks before her body was found. Six torturous weeks of uncertainty. Six weeks of nothing feeling normal. My superhuman strength was beginning to crumble by Sunday 2nd March 2014. I do have spiritual beliefs and there were some very odd moments during those six weeks. The butterfly that appeared in the sitting room when the police first arrived to take notes about my missing daughter. The strangest feeling of Megan resting her head on my shoulder and saying 'Oh, Mummy' as, out of sight from other people, I washed up mugs and felt overwhelmed by a sudden wave of fear and sadness. The feeling that the horses I was working with could feel my surreal calmness and that Megan was with me, with those horses and seeing my world through my eyes.

We had 'closure' at last. I was advised not to identify her. I felt that my chance to say goodbye had been stolen from me and still regret not going to the hospital to do that. The funeral arrangements were overwhelming but we all just kept plodding on with things, putting together music, photographs and talking to our lovely vicar, who really didn't know what to say to me as I was back in superhuman mode, calm and composed, taking control and making sure that Megan would have a beautiful send off.

Which it was. It was beautiful and if she could have seen how many people were there to say goodbye and celebrate her life, then she would have giggled, dipped her head to one side the way she did in her shy manner and probably looked awkward, then given everyone her dazzling blue-eyed smile.

There were butterflies that day, in the church, and everyone commented on how they behaved. A tiny one landed right in front of me on a prayer book and then appeared to lead me out of the church, attached to the vicar's robe. At the time all those little signs felt important.

My proactive, or instrumental grieving started very soon after the funeral. I've heard someone recently describe that feeling as having crusader energy. I was the crusader who would do anything to keep my daughter's memory alive and stop anyone else dying in such a needless, horrific way. No one was allowed to bring their crusade anywhere near my crusade. York was my battlefield and Megan was going to change the way forward for young people in that city. That might all sound crazy, but that must have also been part of the resilience, shining through the tattered shreds of normality that were holding me upright.

Somehow, to survive such devastating loss, one has to find a way of channelling all the accompanying feelings. I think I was suffering from PTSD to some degree as I had strong fight or flight tendencies which didn't really settle down for about two years; I'm not sure they will ever go entirely as I still have the urge to just run away from things sometimes. Working with organisations such as the York Rescue Boat, putting pressure on City of York Council to uphold their side of the river improvements and becoming an ambassador for the Royal Life Saving Society gave me the outlet I needed so desperately so I could use those feelings towards something positive.

I'm a creative person with a tendency towards depression sometimes, which is something I'm well aware of but I'm determined not to get the better of me, because I also have a great need to be a positive person. Being a positive thinking person in the face of intangible grief was a challenge but, and this is where channelling those feelings into action really helped, it was somehow possible to be making something good happen because the love I have for my daughter had to go somewhere. What is stronger than a mother's love for her child? When a child dies, that love doesn't just disappear. I'll never stop feeling that love and I have a strong sense that Megan's love for me and the rest of her family will always be around us.

Life goes on for those left behind. I don't expect I will ever be free of pain but my strong belief in Megan's spirit has kept me going and inspired me along the way. She always wanted me to be happy about things, so I uphold her wishes and try my hardest to be that way.

It is not always possible, and I have very dark days and dark moments; I feel angry, I feel guilty, I miss her so very much; just writing those words makes me cry. I miss her, and all she would have become and I miss the friendship that was developing as she grew up. I just miss her; it hurts like hell and I know I've had to become an even stronger person because of it.

My proactive grieving continued through my work for the Royal Life Saving

Society. A great part of that role was helping to develop a campaign aimed predominantly at young people, especially students, who were at risk of putting themselves in danger whilst out drinking. The effects of prevention work are not that tangible but at this stage, just the fact that Megan's legacy lives on in doing something worthwhile gave me a sense of purpose. I couldn't say when the feeling of being anchored back in January 2014 started to shift slightly, but I no longer feel that it's wrong to move forward and whatever direction my life takes me in I have the comforting feeling that I carry my daughter with me wherever I go. It is said that grief does not get smaller; you, or your life gets bigger. The grief hits me still and there is never a day where I am not aware of how different I feel in myself now. I think there must be a massive readjustment in oneself to be able to cope with such a life changing loss. In some ways I am a better person and in other ways I feel smaller.

My beautiful girl is no longer with us in this world, but I am sure that wherever her spirit is, it is as light as a butterfly and full of light. As the song goes 'the world was never meant for one as beautiful as you.'"

Written in memory of Megan Elizabeth Roberts 16.09.1993 – 23.01.14

The RLSS nominated Jackie for a Yorkshire Woman of Achievement Award in 2016. She said at the time, *"I never thought in a million years that I would win.*

There were so many women there who had done such amazing things. But when they started to describe the winner, I realised they were talking about me." Jackie won the Jane Tomlinson Woman of Courage Award. *"Jane was such an amazing woman and I had met Mike a few times before and I was on his table on the night. To win the award in her name meant so much to me."*

It is typical of Jackie's modesty to play down the honour of receiving this well-deserved award. She said,

"I don't believe anyone who has lost a child or other loved one and follows a path of instrumental grieving, ever expects any acknowledgement for what they're doing as, to my mind anyway, it's simply channelling the love and therefore the grief into doing something positive. I feel that working with RLSS has given me a new sense of purpose which helps me to cope with the loss of the beautiful soul that was my daughter."

Another connection that has come about since James died is via Linda Sewell, whom as I have related before, lost her son Tom in New Zealand.

Linda learned of the loss of Elizabeth Bond's daughter Sarah and reached out to her early on in her grief. I have met Elizabeth a few times and I am struck by her feisty, positive attitude that accords with her views on resilience. She describes it thus:

"When applied to people, this term is what we use to describe how we 'bounce back' or re-form our lives after life changing or devastating events. It's a term we hear a lot today, as opposed to the 'getting on with it' mantra of previous generations. Are these in any way similar? is a question I ask myself frequently.

Growing up in the East End of London in the 1960s where 'the war' and 'the blitz' were still spoken about as recent events (which I guess if you had lived through them, they were) we played on bomb sites and debris that had

remained untouched for over a decade; nonetheless conversations about death and loss were surprisingly scarce.

Looking back, I can only imagine that the pain and disbelief of what so many had lived through had left survivors in a 'shock' that could never have been put into words. My mum told countless stories of people she had grown up with who were no longer around.

My mum had lost her nineteen-year-old brother at Dunkirk and from the day her mum received the letter to inform her that her son was 'missing, believed killed in action' – she never mentioned his name again. My Grandmother died a few years later, still a young woman, having borne this agony without ever sharing it.

I have often thought that my generation, having been brought up by parents who had survived a World War were perhaps given a unique 'set of tools' to guide us into what was, after all a brave new world of peace and prosperity. For me 'getting on with it' was something of the buzzword of my youth. Losing several Aunts and Uncles during my formative years did nothing to prepare me for the sudden loss of my Dad when I was fourteen. This was my introduction to life-changing loss. Subsequently over the years having lost my mum, close family members, one of my best friends and even, tragically a six-year-old nephew....... still nothing prepared me for the shock of the policeman at the door bringing news of my twenty-three-year-old daughter Sarah's fatal accident.

Sarah was less than two weeks into a ten-month working holiday starting in New Zealand. She planned to move on to Australia and eventually make her way home via Fiji.

After a short stay with a friend in Auckland, Sarah joined 'The Kiwi Experience' for an adventurous tour. Whilst on a sedate quadbike tour of the caves and countryside, Sarah lost control of the vehicle and left the track, plunging thirty metres into a ravine. There are more issues here than I am able to articulate. The lack of training, the lack of health and safety guidelines, etc; the list is endless....... Suffice to say that as if the immeasurable loss of our daughter and sister wasn't enough, the ongoing issues and trying to raise awareness was an endurance test too far.

I couldn't possibly talk about resilience without this preamble into what makes me who I am today. I honestly don't know if having the ability to sit here and put this into words eight years on from the loss of our beautiful Sarah is resilience or my very early grounding in the belief that we had to 'get on with it.'

There is no doubt in my mind that were it not for the support network I am blessed with I would never have made it out of those dark, early days when anything other than the physical and mental pain we (me, my husband Jack and two other beautiful daughters, Caroline and Alexandra) were coping with wasn't featuring in our minds. The usually reassuring mundanity of daily life was only to be endured as a step to get us through to the next day.

In the very early days of our grief, Jack and I used the 'sink or swim' analogy. We agreed that 'sinking' was not an option. All things considered, it's clear that for much of the time we are merely 'treading water' but it beats 'sinking.'

So let's suppose that 'resilience' is the modern day 'getting on with it.' Our twenty first century lives certainly give us more scope to find all the help we *need. Whilst everybody still grieves in their own personal way; time won't change that. Now, at least it is acceptable to be open and seek out ways to cope with the pain of immeasurable loss.*

My own lifeline was handed to me when only days after my daughter's death, I was contacted by another very recently bereaved mum. Having read about Sarah's accident and its similarities to her son Tom's fatal accident, Linda found the strength to email me. Having someone to talk to whose position is so similar to your own is immensely valuable, not that for one second we want anybody else to be experiencing this torture. Linda and I have become firm friends. We are both aware that were it not for our tragic stories, our paths may never have crossed but that doesn't stop me feeling grateful for having her in my much-altered life.

The need to have things to look forward to and planning and enjoying events is often seen as part of our rehabilitation. For me personally, getting up and painting on the face I show to the world is what gets me through each day.

I go to work and I guess this is where the 'getting on with it' kicks in. As a rule, no matter how friendly or sympathetic workmates are, without the facade I wouldn't survive the day.

I always remove myself from conversations that I find remotely upsetting — I cannot expect people to censor what they talk about because of my sensitivities. I seriously think that we have to protect and be kind to ourselves. Most importantly be aware of our limitations. Living with the aftermath of unimaginable loss requires some understanding of your own needs.

Being resilient when your life has changed beyond recognition is a huge expectation of yourself. To my mind anything you can achieve that approaches 'normality' shows some resilience. We are only human. Resilience doesn't need to be absolute!"

Elizabeth's words are well considered and reflect her gutsy determination to get through her grief for her daughter in the best ways she knows how.

I cannot write about resilience without including another reference to Sheridan Voysey in regard to his previously mentioned book, *Resilient*.

Sheridan argues that it is not enough simply to hear or read about how we should become resilient, we must act it and we must live it for it to become part of us.

In other words, don't just *talk the talk* but *walk the walk* too.

Sheridan describes four main factors of resilience that are referred to as forms of fitness:

The first factor is emotional fitness, the ability to amplify positive emotions like peace, gratitude, hope, or love, while managing negative ones like bitterness, sadness, or anger. The second is family fitness, developing strong marriages and relationships by building trust, managing conflict, and extending forgiveness. The third is social fitness, having good friendships and work relations by developing empathy and emotional intelligence. And the fourth is spiritual fitness, defined as a sense of meaning and purpose from serving something greater than ourselves.

I would add healing fitness as an important factor in

attaining the resilience to cope with trauma, grief, loss and life's myriad challenges. By healing fitness, I mean the two-way process of healing. This encompasses the healing received from others' thoughts and prayers and the healing that in turn we give out, through our own compassion and empathy for individuals in their times of need.

Sometimes it is difficult to find the time and space in our busy lives to think about healing, whether it is for ourselves or others, and I have come to learn over recent years how important it is to make time, to create time, to take time out, for focusing on introspective thoughts, prayers and healing imagery. I would argue that healing fitness does not depend on following a particular faith or creed, though we need to have in place some form of underlying belief system. At the very least, we must believe in the power of positive thought for any healing to take place, whether it is physical, mental or emotional. Healing fitness is vital for the trinity of contented mind, body and spirit that is reflected in our sense of balance and wellbeing.

We are all spiritual beings, but our spiritual aspects are not always as close to the surface as perhaps they should be. Reaching in and exploring our own spirituality can be a daunting prospect but it is ultimately rewarding, particularly if we can open our hearts to receive the wisdom and guidance of others who have trodden the path we may decide to follow. And if we are not followers of God, or if we are just beginning to explore that road, and if we find the prospect overwhelming ... then the guidance of those who are showing us the route will be appreciated in whatever forms their teachings take.

Resilience plays an important part not just in the grieving process, but in life itself. Resilience provides us with the ability to bounce back from those times when we are at our lowest ebb; thus, we continue to hold hope for improvement, or a better life.

Resilience

Do not speak to me of bravery
For I am not a person brave
Instead, I have been gifted resilience
Against the shocks of life experience

I am blessed with the tenacity
And will to speak out with veracity
I tell it from the heart, lay it straight
All to the point, with considered debate

If, in grief and sorrow, one gets mired
Provocative thought is the outcome desired
Because thought uplifts and gives one reasons

To live with joy through time and seasons

It's not for me to weep and wail
No wasting energy; nor at the Fates to rail
I turn those tears to a healing aid
Resilience means I'm no longer afraid

Ask me not if I am better
There is no simple cure in word and letter
But years dilute the crying inside
And resilience is the salve applied

I call upon those unseen for support
From God to angels to power of thought
Reaching out to the realms, earthly and divine
For the strength that heals the losses of mine

The learning curve is steep, but free
It is there for all, not just for me
Query not how it arrives
Resilience supports, with work it thrives

And should I waver in my fortitude
Resilience is the rock to give me attitude
Grief is a lifestyle, not a choice
Hope and resilience give it strong voice

The teachings of faith are indirect and subtle
I question them without fear of rebuttal
By trusting the guidance that comes from above
My knowledge is fed by honesty and love

Resilience is that immeasurable bounce
that brings me back to upright stance
With prayer and hope I accept my gifts
And in doing so, my spirit lifts

Does resilience bring acceptance?
If that happens, it's not by chance
It seems to me that resilience is Life
Lessons, learned through knocks and strife

Speak to me then of hope; I will respond
Seeking positivity on earth and beyond
Exploring new ways to weather the storm
Resilience... now that is my life's norm.

Andrea Corrie   January 2016

Chapter 11
A Joyful Life

I have seen the sun break through
to illuminate a small field
for a while, and gone my way
and forgotten it. But that was the pearl
of great price, the one field that had
treasure in it. I realize now
that I must give all that I have
to possess it. Life is not hurrying
on to a receding future, nor hankering after
an imagined past. It is the turning
aside like Moses to the miracle
of the lit bush, to a brightness
that seemed as transitory as your youth
once, but is the eternity that awaits you.
The Bright Field by R S Thomas[1]

I wonder whether Shaun and I would have had the idea of taking in lodgers if it had not been for the loss of James. Despite visits from the family, we were rattling round in a house that was too large for us. Over the course of several years, we welcomed Lucy, followed by Jules and Kyle, and then Rachel until we were ready to downsize in 2012.

Each of our lodgers brought many positive elements to our lives over that time and there was laughter in our home once again.

Lucy, my late friend Sylvi's daughter, is a longstanding family friend and she became the catalyst for our becoming more sociable in the ensuing weeks and months through her lively, warm presence in our home.

Grief is a dreadful confidence sapper and we needed the restorative presence of other people to relearn how to be more outgoing.

Lucy started this process and when she moved on, we were confident enough to advertise for lodgers whom we didn't know; it was a rewarding experience to get acquainted with them.

Jules and Kyle brought a vivacity and sense of fun to the house during their time with us; it was lovely that they felt able to introduce us to their friends and we had some fun evenings round the dinner table. Rachel too became a friend rather than just someone renting a room and we felt very blessed with the experiences we had with all these individual residents of our house.

I was very anxious about relocating to a new house before we moved to Knaphill in 2012. Having lived in Addlestone for many years and been surrounded by my family memories on a daily basis, it was strange to think we would be in an area where we did not know anybody. Geographically our move was only eight miles, but it took me out of all the attachments and comfort zones that I already knew. But I need not have worried - not least because there was a sense of bringing James with us even though he would not know our new home ... one of the first things I did was to put up his photograph on the windowsill and it never felt strange that he did not live there with us.

We quickly made friends through our local pub. I must stress that making new friendships is another really important development that comes with being further along the grief line. At first you are entirely closed in upon yourself, and making friends, unless they are fellow bereaved parents, seems too difficult a prospect. Gradually you begin to feel that you are shining a welcoming light again and the response is that people are once more drawn to you. It is a mirror effect that results from your body language, expression, appearance and general mien.

We have been very fortunate in recent years to meet others who, as they have come to know us better, feel able to ask questions about James, empathise with us and not be made uncomfortable by our situation. They are not bereaved parents and never met James, but they all have an understanding of trauma.

You learn that we each have our own story and it is easy to forget that other people go through 'stuff' too.

In return I think we have become more outgoing and appreciative of what is around us, living each day as fully as we can. I have a sense of living my days as usefully as I can manage. As my dad used to say of life, *"This is the play, not the dress rehearsal."*

New environments bring their own challenges. Each new place or experience, be it work or social, always brings with it the potential awkwardness of how, when and whether you are going to be sharing your story. I have to remind myself that I do not visibly wear my grief.

Also, it is quite liberating to be in an environment where nobody knows what has happened. I always have to weigh up whether or not it is appropriate to bring my story to the table, as it were. The feeling that I might be judged or labelled by my tragedy, forever known as 'that poor woman who lost her son' is not a pleasant one. In social situations, the awkwardness created if I tell strangers what has happened, people's inevitable shocked reaction and their ensuing questions, or the difficult silences that follow, make it easier to say nothing, until or unless I am sufficiently comfortable in the environment and confident of the responses I may receive.

I want to keep the memory of James alive and I do so in

a multitude of significant ways: by writing about grief; by campaigning for safety in the water; by public speaking. But it saddens me that we have not yet evolved a way of talking about the children we have lost in casual, social situations. If we do so, it is considered an imposition. Rudeness almost. It kills the conversation stone dead. My aim is to develop an etiquette of bereavement, a set of simple rules which causes the least upset for both the parent who has lost a child and the listener.

It is, of course, a truism, but only parents who have lost a child can understand the profound depth of the grief; the sense that the natural order has been disrupted and life will never again resume its old course.

I have thought long and hard about how best to break the taboo, about finding the right balance when talking about loss and responding to it.

I believe the best reaction is both simple and understated. If a parent tells you their child has died, simply respond that you're very sorry to hear it. And if you want to know what happened, just ask them. Know too, that no offence will be taken if you don't.

I heard a brilliant example of how best to be a friend to someone who is newly bereaved. Actions speak louder than words and, in these circumstances, it was Sam Rayburn, a former long-time Speaker of the House of Representatives in the USA who revealed himself as a true friend.

One night, the teenage daughter of a neighbour of Speaker Rayburn died suddenly. Early the next morning the grieving father heard a knock at his door. When he opened it, there stood Speaker Rayburn. Rayburn said, *"I just came by to see what I could do to help."* The father replied, *"I don't think there is anything you can do, Mr Speaker. We are making all the arrangements."*

"Well," said Mr Rayburn, *"have you had your coffee this morning?"* The man replied that the family had not even thought about breakfast. So, Mr Rayburn said that he could at least make something for them to eat and drink. While he was working in the kitchen, the father came in and said, *"Mr Speaker, I thought you were supposed to be having breakfast at the White House this morning?"*

"Well, I was," Mr. Rayburn said, *"but I called the President and told him I had a friend who was in trouble and I couldn't come."*

We moved house again in 2017, this time heading west to mid Devon and a massive change in all areas of our lives. Shaun retired at the end of 2016 and I left my post at a local GP practice in March 2017. The adjustment to a new area and lifestyle took some time to achieve and it was not without its difficulties. In particular my brother Peter, who was diagnosed with cancer in 2014, became more significantly unwell soon after our move. It is ironic in that we had just become neighbours living in the same county and were also enjoying a harmonious relationship. But unfortunately, his health went downhill rapidly, and he died in November 2017. This loss, though it was expected, left me feeling particularly bereft.

In recent years, Peter and I had a new, closer connection as adult siblings.

For once, I was proud to say, *"I am catching up with my brother next week,"* rather than pretending he didn't exist because he was so annoying. He was invited and present at two significant family occasions - a special birthday and Christmas 2016.

We finally talked about the loss of our parents and of James and were able to cry and laugh together as never before, despite the sadness.

I carry with me those memories, and the memories of some happy childhood times too. I also have the joy of continued contact with Peter's former partner, Liz and her son, my lovely nephew Ben. Liz lives a scant hour away and although Ben is currently travelling and working in Australia, we keep in touch with a closeness that was not present before.

Lizzie, Ben and I can share reminiscences of the complex character that was Peter.

We can laugh about shared recollections and we can create new memories by spending time together, although he has gone. We are able to honour his memory in a variety of ways. We can recall his intelligence, his linguistic abilities and his love of (some pretty strange!) music.

All these are therapeutic elements in the grieving process.

And there is of course the catharsis of writing which seems to be a family trait, judging by this wonderful contribution from Ben, who graduated from University with a First-Class Honours degree in English in 2018:

"On being asked to contribute to this book, I asked myself how I could position my own experience alongside Andrea's, given the gravity of what she has had to deal with in losing a child compared to my, perhaps more commonplace, loss of a parent. Having mentally gone back and forth about what I could possibly write, worrying that my loss is somehow not enough, I realised why my aunt asked me to write in the first place.

It is cathartic to write. Putting my thoughts onto paper has been an important factor in helping me to understand the different stages of my own grieving process, reflecting on my father's life in a shining light. I am currently keeping both a travel journal and blog; in them, references to my old man often surface without me consciously making them. Disregarding the anxious inhibitions that have pickpocketed me of my voice in the past has been liberating and through prose, I have been able to learn about the person grief has made me. Of losing my Grandma Dot (her mother), Andrea writes 'there was the woman I was before, and the woman I was afterwards.' I have noticed a

278

similar pattern since losing Dad.

In losing the man who I looked up to as a boy, I have found myself to be searching for him within myself. I am unsure as to whether the loss has triggered certain habits that remind me of him, or I have always had these habits but they are merely amplified now he is gone. From my use of phrases I associate with him, to his dry sense of humour, I see more of Dad in my character all the time. I miss the man I knew but am constantly reminded that he is a part of me. I travel as he travelled, charm as he charmed and smile as he smiled.

Nearly three years after his cancer diagnosis in 2014, Dad's physical and mental health deteriorated suddenly. Around my twenty-first birthday, as he strong-armed me into taking him to Israel on a trip that I believe pushed him beyond his limits, he left a coming of age mark on me that I will never shake off, passing away just two days after our return. It takes immense mental energy to transform the negative emotions associated with grief and trauma into something positive, but my aunt has demonstrated her ability to do this in the face of all adversity. Her ongoing work with the RNLI and other organisations is an example of the constructive, practical ways in which she is making a difference, whilst her writing poignantly offers comfort and support to all those who have experienced loss.

Andrea has been, and will remain to me, a remarkable role model. To have such a strong woman as the closest immediate family on my Dad's side has been a blessing. Our 'new closeness' she notes since my father's death is an example of her ability to constantly find each cloud's silver lining. Ours is a positive relationship that has flourished because of a negative event. This closeness has indeed been crucial for me in working through my own grief for Dad.

In her, not only do I see a resilient and inspiring individual, but I see the intelligence and attention to detail her brother possessed. If, in sharing, my voice can make anywhere near the impact hers has had on me, I am content that my writing has had its desired effect. She was there for me in a way nobody else was in Dad's final weeks, present on the day he passed and since then I have followed her from shrouds of darkness to a place of mourning light. For that, I am eternally grateful."

The cold, dreary weather and a feeling of isolation from my hitherto local support network made our first winter in Devon a difficult time. Joy seemed to be in short supply at that time, but it was hardly surprising.

I am pleased to say that once Christmas and the new year had been and gone, I felt much better in myself and more inclined to notice the small joys that can be had, for example, from the sight of the first snowdrops pushing through the cold soil.

There are times when communicating with my own grief pushes aside other priorities and I have found it is best to sit with it and just let it take the place it wants to. Some time ago, I had a day like that, and I wrote:

"I don't know why, but today feels like a day for remembering. It's not an anniversary, or a birthday, or a special day for any particular reason. But I feel like I've been so caught up in the here and now, so busy assimilating all the new experiences of our first Spring living in the Devon countryside, that somehow my remembrance of James has slipped down the page.

How's that for an admission? I can almost hear a sharp intake of breath from the recently bereaved.

"What did you say? You can't be a very good mother. How can you possibly forget? How can you not be thinking of your son every waking moment?"

Well, hang on a moment, don't get too carried away. Is it so wrong after more than a decade, to allow myself to shrug off the mantle of grief now and then? Is it wrong not to feel guilty for doing so? Letting go is not the same as forgetting.

Perhaps it's time for a chat with James to clarify things.

"Gee, thanks, Mum, nice of you to tell the world you're forgetting all about me."

"Now, I didn't say that, did I?"

"No, but you implied it. Are you, as they say, 'over it'?"

"Never, James. I can never be 'over it.'

Let me tell you how it is.

How could I forget 19, nearly twenty years of your life with us? Those 19 years still underpin everything I see and do. Trust me James, I don't waste my days, and do you know why I don't waste my days?"

"Is it because you feel you're always having to make up for me not being there, or is that too vain?"

"Very mature observation, son. You've obviously grown more sensible now that you are in your thirties!

No … I don't feel that I have to make up for your not being here, in the same way I don't want anyone else who knows and loves you to feel that.

But and it is a big but, any parent who has lost a child, indeed anyone who has lost anyone close, will live differently to a new default setting. We must value the life we have left, for none of us knows how long that may be …

After all, we have a better understanding of how life can be snatched away in an instant."

"I think I get that mum. Are you happy these days, would you say?"

"Yes, son, I can truly say I have attained proper happiness again. It has taken a long time. It has taken a lot of working through the trauma, distress, shock and pain of grief. But the joys in life seem heightened when I allow myself to really embrace them."

"How have you arrived at that point, mum?"

"Wow, James it has taken so many different directions to reach the place that is comfortable, it would take an age to list them all.

But most importantly, I have had to learn to trust in the renewal of optimism and positivity.

I have had to learn to have faith that things will get better.

I have learned that I can step out of the darkness, into the mourning light."

"Do you still see things that jog you into memories of me, Mum?"

"Yes, of course I do. Why only today, I was in a shop and I saw one of those wooden artist's mannequins, you remember you had one? You can pose it into different positions and draw it …Something like that takes me back instantly to remembering you. Whatever else might change, those memory jogs certainly don't. And of course, some music always takes me back immediately."

"Ok, you're beginning to convince me."

"It's simple, really. I know that by remembering you, you are with me always. But like I don't need to be in a Church in order to pray, I don't need to be remembering you every moment in obvious ways …"

"What do you mean?"

"Well, if I am out walking, I will see something that makes me think of you and smile. You know we moved to Devon in 2017 and the road we use most frequently takes us through a village called Bolham. I can imagine you … you would have called it Gollum, or Bottom, just to make me laugh. I can picture that. Those sorts of personal memories are very special."

"I'm glad you are happy, mum. I'm sorry not to be there to share more stuff with you but I am pleased that you can enjoy life in a new way. Does anyone in Devon know about me, by the way?"

"Ah, that's an interesting question. You will recall that at the start, I wanted to tell anybody and everybody. These days I am more selective, and I choose whom to share you with.

I've made a new friend, and I told her recently, because I knew she wouldn't react negatively … some people can't handle others' 'stuff' – but she gets it. And that's comforting. I will always need a variety of go-to people, and what is interesting that many of them never met you, but they all feel they know you!"

"That's good to hear, mum. I am glad I left my mark."

"James, you have no idea. Sometimes on a clear night I look up to the skies and marvel at the stars. You are one of those stars, and your light shines brightly in all those whom you left behind, with love, and optimism.

My appreciation for your life, transforms the years since your passing into something bearable. I hold what was so precious and special in the past as treasure deep within my heart and soul.

This is my truth and certainty at today's point in the process of living with loss. So, even if you aren't top of my 'to do' list every day, rest assured you'll never be forgotten. Got the picture?"

"I get that Mum, thanks for checking in with me. Talk again soon. Love you."

"Love you all the world, James."

When you are grieving or working through a stressful situation, you often hear the phrase 'new normality.'

I was reminded of this when I read a column in the local paper by Revd Andy Humm, the vicar of St George and St Paul's, the church in Tiverton that I attend.

Andy pointed out how the concept of normality has changed, using as an example the way we carry out research today. It is less common for us to go to the library to explore reference books such as the tome-like Encyclopaedia Britannica than it is for us to just 'Google it'!

Talking about being with bereaved families planning a funeral or in other circumstances, he went on to say,

"... I try to get families to talk about a new normal. This is because the reality of the situation they find themselves in, means they cannot go back to how it was. The person they loved has died, or the situation has meant that things cannot be the same. Yet tomorrow will come, and the day has to be lived in the light of what has happened, a new normal."

It's an interesting choice of words ... 'in the light of what has happened' ... for when I talk about new normality since losing James in 2005, I invariably describe it as living in the mourning light. That has become normal for me.

But there are other, more recent losses that have necessarily become included in my new normality.

As I wrote in Chapter 6, in 2016 I lost one of my longest-standing friends to cancer. I had known Sylvi thirty years. I have learned that to lose a close friend is to lose a person with whom you have shared all your secrets. You have grown together as you have trodden through your life, whatever its experiences.

The new normal of living without her does not take away the memories, or the sadness of missing her.

Then in 2017, I lost my only brother Peter, also to cancer. He was 65. To lose a brother is to lose someone with whom you thought you would grow old, regardless of your relationship. I think I am only just beginning to process these losses and to assimilate them into new normality. Sometimes it is the little things you miss the most. I know I miss seeing their handwriting in letters and cards.

Whenever I see hydrangeas, I think of Sylvi. Whenever I hear David Bowie's music, I think of Peter. These are small but important ingredients in new normality. Anyone who has lost someone will recognise their own personal triggers.

What astounds me is the adaptability and fluidity that we all possess that allows us to accommodate change and to slot it into our everyday lives.

We learn to absorb hurt; to grow a carapace around ourselves that shields our hearts from the pain of grief and loss. When we are strong enough, we look out towards the light again and create our new normality.

Aspects of new normality can, of course, be positive rather than negative. It is my new normal to enjoy living in the countryside and to have been able to choose to work again after a lengthy sabbatical; both of which are true blessings.

The tangled skeins of lives and relationships offer endless opportunities for us to learn, shift our thinking, recognise what is calling us the loudest and respond to it. My biggest shift in new normality occurred thanks to the Alpha course in 2016. My old normal of believing there was 'something out there, not sure what', and enjoying practices such as complementary, holistic therapies and meditation, now sit comfortably alongside Christian worship.

My life in the mourning light now contains an additional shining light and it is a joy to continue to explore and learn more about this new normal.

I am always looking for new, different ways to process my sadness with a productive result that preferably benefits others as well as myself.   It seems to me that learning, seeking out knowledge, the discipline of study and expanding education are some of the most helpful ways of processing grief.

I enjoy the resultant sharing of what I have learned, through the written and spoken word.

A new joy in our lives is that of Shadow, the canine addition to our family who brought with him a whole raft of happiness. Whether you are experiencing grief of not, it is well recognised that pets improve your sense of wellbeing.

Shaun and I had already established that getting a dog was part of our plan when we moved to Devon. We wanted to give purpose to our walks and exploration of the countryside. And of course, a dog helps you to be sociable, as you invariably chat with other dog owners when you are out and about.

We envisaged homing a compact canine who would slot easily into our new surroundings, but trawls of general rescue centres did not yield any suitable pooches.

I eventually found my way to the website of Forever Hounds Trust. This is an excellent charity that rehomes unwanted, abused or abandoned greyhounds and lurchers; and we put our name down for a cat-friendly hound (a bit of a tall order for dogs that generally have a very high prey drive!). However, after a relatively short time, and a thorough home check, we were contacted about a four-year-old pure-bred greyhound called Snowie. This handsome black and white chap had quite a chequered history. He was not an ex racer, as many greyhounds are, but had been rescued from living on an allotment in the North of England. Sadly, his owner died, and the family could not take on the dogs he owned, so he came into the care of the Trust. After a while in kennels he was rehomed with a family who had both dogs and cats. All seemed well, but unfortunately one of the other dogs became ill and the owner had to return Snowie to kennels. One sunny day in April 2018, three lovely Forever Hounds Trust ladies arrived at our house, with this very large, lanky, anxious looking dog.

We carefully brought the cats, Minstrel and Daisy, into the same room under supervision; Snowie passed his 'tolerating cats' test with flying colours, and after a week's trial of our fostering him, he very quickly walked into our lives and crept into our hearts.

He was soon renamed Shadow due to his following my every move – particularly in the early days when he was settling into his pampered Devon life. He takes up residence on the sofa whenever possible (a very typical greyhound trait) and he makes us smile on a daily basis.

There is evidence that pets improve our mood by increasing a variety of feelgood chemicals in our brains (dopamine, oxytocin, serotonin).

In terms of processing feelings of grief, I believe that Shadow plays an important part. When you are grieving, you need to channel elsewhere the love you gave to those you have lost. It is easy to humanise your pets, and get to know their unique personalities, so why should you not lavish them with love and affection? Distraction is an important part of the grieving process, too. The bereaved often need to find an alternative focus to distract from constantly dwelling on sadness and a dog certainly fulfils this role; if you are ready for the responsibility.

I feel the timing of our getting Shadow was just right for us.

Shadow and the cats are entirely non-judgmental. There is an absence of expectation from animals (apart from at food or walk time!) that makes it easy for you to relate to them.

They don't need you to act a certain way or talk a certain way. They often pick up when you are feeling sad and can be extra affectionate, sensing your need for comfort. When you are happy, so are they.

I won't play down the responsibility that comes with having a dog in the family (not least picking up after them) – naturally there are costs associated with them for feeding and vet bills (insurance is definitely worth having for an accident-prone hound). There is no doubt they are a tie when it comes to planning holidays and trips away; but all these things add up to a total small price to pay, for the life-enhancing joy they bring simply through their loving, affectionate and loyal presence. Shadow has become part of the family in an undemanding yet rewarding way.

One advantage of having the distance of a number of years since James died is the renewed ability to relish happy events without feeling guilty. There is always a sense of wistful regret that he is not here to share our happy times, but it is possible now to accept the fact of his absence in a way that sits more comfortably.

We have shared in our granddaughters' and our grandson's birthday celebrations. How good it felt! - to smile and laugh and watch the children playing together, the adults sharing conversation without feeling that they need to walk on eggshells around us or fearing they might say the wrong thing.

What a delight it is to be laying down new family memories that are evidenced by the joyful images and videos from our phones and cameras.

We are secure enough with our memories to know that no-one has forgotten James. We can speak his name more freely without fear of upsetting ourselves or others. The poignancy of his absence is less painful.

I am happy for all our children and extended family that we can feel more relaxed about family conviviality these days.

I am happy that each of our children goes on with their productive lives without a constant cloud of distress hanging over them and we do not feel the need to keep going over the old ground, although we can talk about James when we want to.

We can say wistfully, *"James would have loved this, James would have laughed at that ..."* without distress, rather with a deep sense of underlying sadness.

At first it is almost impossible not to be conscious of the absence of that person who should be there but isn't. It is unfair, unjust and untimely.

But it is what it is ....and accepting that which we cannot change is the hard part.

It is all too easy for me to imagine that people think to

themselves … 'She must be over it by now, after all it is all these years since it happened ...'

To those people, I say, I will never be *over it*.

I can never accept that my son died due to accident before he had a chance to live his adult life.

What I **can** accept however, is that James lived his allotted life span, he lived it to the full, his memory lives on in many, many minds, and I will never, ever regret having had the opportunity to be his mother for nineteen years and ten months. I knew my son; after all we shared a body for nine months before he was born! – and I know that even now, part of him resides within me.

I feel regret for the future that he cannot have. I hold regret on behalf of all the members of our family and friends who love and miss him, but I do not regret the past, and all the memories it holds.

Joy is a nebulous concept; its moments are often fleeting but they are precious, nonetheless. Within my family, I witness joy. When our grandson Charlie has stayed with us for a few days, we generally meet with Stella halfway between our home and theirs for the handover. A five-year-old at the time of writing, Charlie is a delightful, lively little boy. When he sees Stella's car arrive in the car park, something wonderful happens.

His eyes light up and a wide grin fills his face. He almost fizzes with excitement as she parks the car. She walks towards him, her face also alight with a beaming smile. *"Mummy!"* he cries, and leaps into her arms. *"Charlie! did you miss me?"* Their faces, so similar, are alight with a joyous love that is heart-warming to see. It is joy personified and I am blessed to witness it.

Living in the mourning light brings its own particular brand of joy. It has taken up residence in my heart and pushed aside the fear that lingered so closely behind it. This has not been a quick process. When I completed writing *Into the Mourning Light* five years ago, in hindsight I believe that I was only just beginning to live in the mourning light.

I now have a better understanding of that particular place. It is a resurrection of sorts. The dawning of mourning light is only possible after the darkest of darkness ...it is the obverse side to despair and its light grows bright and true. At the time of writing, it is fourteen years since James died. I cannot pinpoint when there was a change in direction in the mourning light that really guided me towards joy but guide it did. I feel the embrace of joy with only the smallest of reservations today.

I offer heartfelt gratitude to each of the many contributors who generously continue to shape my new life in the mourning light.

Today, after these years of loss, I can say to James,

"My son, you are missed as much as ever. You are loved as greatly now as you were for all the days of your life.

But … I can tell you that I am thankful for all the good things that have happened, and continue to happen, as time passes.

I am thankful to be given the strength and confidence to do so much in your memory. I am thankful to be living in the mourning light.

James. My James.
I say your name,
with joy, not regret,
with pride, not shame,
to remember, not to forget,
with laughter, not tears,
with thoughts of today, not yesterday,
with love for tomorrow and all our tomorrows.

Acknowledgements and Thanks

Each chapter of *Living in the Mourning Light* has been road-tested by a small, select readership drawn from my friends and colleagues. These kind individuals were encouraged to send me their feedback and I am most grateful for their considered, thoughtful and valuable responses which helped to shape the book.

Thank you all.

The list of organisations with whom I have a connection continues to grow; for fear of omitting any I am not listing them, but their presence in the book makes them obvious. Their willingness to share and contribute has undoubtedly been a great boost to the content of both my books.

Thank you to each and every individual I have met who demonstrates sincere passion and commitment to making a difference; attributes I can only applaud and emulate.

In 2014, the completion and publication of *Into the Mourning Light*, which tells James's story and summarises eight years of loss, marked a seminal point for me. Many people played a part in pulling together the strands which eventually led to publication. Their feedback spurred me on to keep writing, not just my blog but this book too. I am grateful to each and every one of the contributors to either or both of my books; not only my steadfast family but also my friends and James's friends.

Thank you, each of you made it possible.

Many of the people whom I have encountered along the way never knew James, but they now know his story. It is a privilege to share him with so many friends.

Thank you, everyone.

"When we honestly ask ourselves which person in our lives means the most to us, we often find that it is those who, instead of giving advice, solutions, or cures, have chosen rather to share our pain and touch our wounds with a warm and tender hand.

The friend who can be silent with us in a moment of despair or confusion, who can stay with us in an hour of grief and bereavement, who can tolerate not knowing, not curing, not healing and face with us the reality of our powerlessness, that is a friend who cares."

Henri J M Nouwen

Citations

Chapter 1
1 Emily Dickinson, *Hope is the Thing With Feathers*; Source: *The Poems of Emily Dickinson Edited by R. W. Franklin*; Harvard University Press, 1999
2 Paulo Coelho, *Adultery*, 2014; Knopf
3 Desmond Tutu, *Desmond Tutu Quotes*: https://www.brainyquote.com/quotes/desmond_ tutu_454129

Chapter 2
1 Hermes Trismegistus: *The Emerald Tablet*
2 Elisabeth Kübler -Ross,1969; *On Death and Dying*; New York: Collier Books

Chapter 3
1 Youtube Video: B3NET Media Group Awareness News Channel, June 2014
2 Stroebe, M.S, and Schut, H.A.W. ,1999; 'The Dual Process Model of Coping with Bereavement: Rationale and Description', *Death Studies*
3 Marcel Proust: *Remembrance of Things Past*

Chapter 4
NONE

Chapter 5
Nb All Biblical references are from www.BibleGateway.com Holy Bible, New International Version®, NIV® Copyright ©1973, 1978, 1984, 2011 by Biblica, Inc.®
1 Judith Tebbut: 2013: A Long Walk Home, One Woman's Story of Kidnap, Hostage, Loss and Survival; Faber and Faber

2   Sheridan Voysey, 2013: *Resurrection Year: Turning Broken Dreams into New Beginnings;* Thomas Nelson

3   Sheridan Voysey, 2015: *Resilient: Your Invitation to a Jesus-shaped Life;* Discovery House

4   Sheridan Voysey, 2019: *The Making of Us: On who we can become when Life Doesn't Go As Planned;* Thomas Nelson

5   See Revelation 12:7

6   See Luke 1:26-38

7   See Psalm 91

8   C S Lewis, 1943: *Mere Christianity*

9   See John 3:3

10   See John 3:8

11   Bear Grylls: Author of *Mud, Sweat and Tears*; Interview with Judith Woods, Daily Telegraph, 30 January 2012

12   Mary Stevenson, 1939: *Footprints in the Sand*

Chapter 6

1   Maya Angelou, 2013: *The Complete Collected Poems of Maya Angelou; Virago*

2   www.wordle.com

3   John Wesley, 1703-1791 *Letters of John Wesley*

4   William Barclay, 1971: *New Testament Words*

5   Raniero Cantalamessa, 2002: *Life in Christ*, Liturgical Press

6   Annie Broadbent, 2017: *Speaking of Death: What the Bereaved Really Need;* Little, Brown

Chapter 7

1   Petrichor Eye on Sky, 2016; *The Times of India* (New Delhi); Mar 17, 2016

2   C S Lewis, 1961: *A Grief Observed*

Chapter 8

1   Danielle Steele, 1996: *The Gift*, Dell
2   Sophocles: *Phaedra, fragment 612*

Chapter 9

1   Christina Rossetti, 1849: *'Remember' in: Goblin market and other poems (1862)*
2   Eleanor Roosevelt: *You Learn by Living: Eleven Keys for a More Fulfilling Life;* Harper Perennial 2011 version
3   Sheridan Voysey, 2015: *Resilient: Your Invitation to a Jesus-shaped Life;* Discovery House

Chapter 10

1   Julian of Norwich, ?1372; *Revelations of Divine Love: Short Text*
2   Jimmy Carter: US President 1977/81

Chapter 11

1   R S Thomas, 1975: *The Bright Field*; *Laboratories of the Spirit*, MacMillan

Abbreviations, organisations and acronyms

TCF	The Compassionate Friends
DSN	Drowning Support Network
RNLI	Royal National Lifeboat Institution
NWSF	National Water Safety Forum
TTWSF	Tidal Thames Water Safety Forum
CRUSE	Bereavement Support
MCA	Maritime and Coastguard Agency
ASA	Amateur Swimming Association
CFOA	Chief Fire Officers' Association
RLSS	Royal Life Saving Society
RoSPA	Royal Society for the Prevention of Accidents
SOBs	Survivors of Bereavement by Suicide
SFRS	Surrey Fire and Rescue Service
LFB	London Fire Brigade
FHT	Forever Hounds Trust

Printed in Great Britain
by Amazon

35072932R00196